DEVIL
ON THE
FRONT
ROW

DEVIL ON THE FRONT ROW

RON SUTTON

CREATION HOUSE

Devil on the Front Row: Seducing Spirits and Doctrines of Demons in the Modern Church
by Ron Sutton
Published by Creation House
A Charisma Media Company
600 Rinehart Road
Lake Mary, Florida 32746
www.charismamedia.com

This book or parts thereof may not be reproduced in any form, stored in a retrieval system, or transmitted in any form by any means—electronic, mechanical, photocopy, recording, or otherwise—without prior written permission of the publisher, except as provided by United States of America copyright law.

Unless otherwise noted, all Scripture quotations are from the Holy Bible, New International Version. Copyright © 1973, 1978, 1984, 2010, 2011, International Bible Society. Used by permission.

Scripture quotations marked GW are from *God's Word*® Translation, ©1995 by God's Word to the Nations. All rights reserved.

Scripture quotations marked KJV are from the King James Version of the Bible.

Scripture quotations marked NKJV are from the New King James Version of the Bible. Copyright © 1979, 1980, 1982 by Thomas Nelson, Inc., publishers. Used by permission.

Scripture quotations marked NLT are from the Holy Bible, New Living Translation, copyright © 1996. Used by permission of Tyndale House Publishers, Inc., Wheaton, IL 60189. All rights reserved.

Publisher's Note: The views expressed in this book are not necessarily the views held by the publisher.

Design Director: Justin Evans
Cover design by Justin Evans

Copyright © 2015 by Ron Sutton
All rights reserved.

Visit the author's website: ronsuttonministries.com.

Library of Congress Cataloging-in-Publication Data: 2015950376
International Standard Book Number: 978-1-62998-484-1
E-book International Standard Book Number:
978-1-62998-485-8

While the author has made every effort to provide accurate telephone numbers and Internet addresses at the time of publication, neither the publisher nor the author assumes any responsibility for errors or for changes that occur after publication.

First edition

15 16 17 18 19 — 9 8 7 6 5 4 3 2 1
Printed in the United States of America

DEDICATION

To my daughter Brianna, a passionate lover of Jesus who worships God in the Spirit and in truth.

CONTENTS

PREFACE: Fire in My Bones xi

CHAPTER 1: Subtle and Seducing Influences 1

CHAPTER 2: Spiritual Specialists 21

CHAPTER 3: Brother Love's Traveling Salvation Show . . . 45

CHAPTER 4: The Seeker-Sensitive Delusion 65

CHAPTER 5: The Return of Cheap Grace 93

CHAPTER 6: Lying Signs and Wonders 105

CHAPTER 7: It's Supernatural, Isn't It? 141

CHAPTER 8: Holy Laughter, Batman! 167

CHAPTER 9: The Catastrophe of Compromise 193

Notes 213

About the Author 219

Contact the Author 221

Preface

FIRE IN MY BONES

I BURIED THIS BOOK long ago. I carefully placed it under several other nearly completed manuscripts and locked the vault. If you are reading these words, you know that it either refused to die or rose from the dead. That doesn't matter now. You are reading it and I can only pray that it doesn't trouble you as it has me. You might consider it irreverent; I slaughter a sacred cow in nearly every chapter. I fear it will cause me to lose friends and infuriate people. That is why I kept it locked up for such a long time.

The thoughts that follow have been paid for with a lot of lost sleep. They have been begging to get out of my head and spill onto these pages for many years. Some started arresting my attention way back in the early days of the Jesus movement over forty years ago; that's when it first dawned on me that even Spirit-filled Christians could be deceived. I was shocked in 1973 when some of my recently converted friends, and some not so recently, left town to join the Children of God cult. I soon learned that it was happening throughout the nation. During those turbulent times other cults appeared, and I wrote a few pamphlets and endeavored to rescue people who had been deceived. I also attempted to warn pastors and churches about the dangers.

Most of my warnings fell on deaf ears. That is why I began seizing new ideas by the throat and locking them up the moment they hit my head. I didn't want them to germinate and lead to a book like this. I didn't want to be labeled an alarmist. I made up my mind not to speak or write about the thoughts that were troubling my mind. But like Jeremiah, I lost the battle: "But if I say, 'I will not mention his word or speak anymore in his name,' his word is in my heart like a fire, a fire shut up in my bones. I am weary of holding it in; indeed, I cannot" (Jer. 20:9, NIV).

A few years later, I became aware of something much more disturbing: seducing spirits were no longer standing outside the churches pulling people away. They moved inside and brought aberrations of the gospel with them, and few even noticed what was happening. The devil started attending churches all over America. In fact, he began to show up at some of the largest ones in the country. In many of them, he could sit on the front row through the entire service and never experience an uncomfortable moment. That disturbed me even more than the cults that came and then left with a few victims. The devil started attending regularly and was not even recognized. He was no longer outside trying to pull people away; he was inside intermingling with careless believers who weren't able to discern his presence.

Satan became even more aggressive during the 1980s. He got to some of the most famous leaders in the church.

They began preaching a materialistic gospel and living as lavishly as kings. There was a strong reaction from some segments, but most didn't seem to mind. They kept burying them in money, even after several were embroiled in moral and financial scandals. And that was just the tip of the iceberg. A lot of other crazy, extrabiblical stuff started taking place. I began to wonder if charismatic Christians had lost their ability to discern between the true and the false.

The tragic mixture of truth and error sweeping through the church deeply troubled me. I felt like Jeremiah with fire shut up in my bones. I had to speak out. But I soon discovered that most people didn't want to hear about false prophets and delusions of the last days. Doors closed to me everywhere. People didn't want to hear warnings of danger and deception. As I began to ponder the reactions to my warnings, it dawned on me just how successful the seducing spirits had been. Their strategy of infiltration had worked well. False prophets were everywhere and almost no one suspected them. If they are polite and smile nicely, nobody dreams they could be a false prophet—much less a wolf in sheep's clothing. They became, dare I say it, quite cozy among us. Famous television preachers got so comfortable they started using all kinds of crazy gimmicks to get money; and people played along with hardly a whimper. They operated like con men; but most pastors didn't warn their people because they didn't want to create controversy by judging or touching "God's anointed" (1 Chron. 15:22; Ps. 105:15).

The gospel was diluted; and sound doctrine took a back seat to extrabiblical revelations, prophecies, and sensational experiences. The greatest danger was no longer cults and false prophets outside the church; it became the seducers who moved in among us with a tragic mixture of truth and error. It was a subtle and pervasive invasion. The watchmen on the walls must have been sleeping. Only a few saw what was happening and sounded the alarm. Some men became famous by cooperating with seducing spirits who taught them how to manipulate a crowd and manufacture a movement. They played with people's emotions and soon all kinds of bizarre manifestations began to occur in big meetings—but many went along with it, even when they started calling the spurious manifestations the outpouring of the Spirit. Some of the false prophets became experts at staging miracles, and a lot of people who knew better pretended not to know what was going on and let them get away with it.

Leaders who remembered how guys like Jeremiah got treated grew more determined not to touch "God's anointed." They stood back and let false prophets tell a watching world that all the weirdness was truly born of the Holy Spirit. Expertly evoked emotional and fleshly eruptions were called manifestations of the Spirit, and people who were looking for a shortcut to revival came to jump in the river. Credible leaders should have confronted the false prophets before they were ever exposed for falsehood and immorality; but confrontation is almost a lost art in the modern church. Many got a pass until scandals erupted around them and brought reproach on all of us. Even after some of them were exposed, charismatic leaders were polite and remained quiet about it. Most of the noise came from leaders who stood outside the charismatic fence.

Our discernment became so clouded and our gospel so diluted, an army of deceivers was able to slip into the mainstream of the Charismatic movement. It became increasingly difficult to distinguish between the true and the false. The Spirit of truth, in some instances, became so grieved He withdrew—and the deluded worshippers didn't even realize He was no longer among them. That's when I started thinking: "The devil could attend some of our meetings, sit on the front row, and never experience an uncomfortable moment." That thought resisted arrest and finally succeeded in releasing all the others locked away deep in my brain. The moment they were free, they joined forces and compelled me to write this book. I completed it long ago but have been reticent to send it to a publisher. If you are reading this, I lost that battle too.

I want to conclude here by acknowledging two men who greatly influenced my life and ministry: Derek Prince and David Wilkerson. I have been drinking at their wells since 1973. They have both graduated to heaven, but being dead they yet speak (Heb. 11:4). If I have retained one shred of sanity after wrestling for so many years with the seducing spirits and doctrines of demons addressed in these pages, I owe it to them. Derek Prince taught me that the Spirit and the Word are always in perfect agreement; one never contradicts the other. David Wilkerson gave me the courage to challenge the false and the conviction to stand for truth—even if doing so left me as lonely as Elijah on top of Mt. Carmel.

Chapter 1

SUBTLE AND SEDUCING INFLUENCES

Now the Spirit expressly says that in latter times some will depart from the faith, giving heed to deceiving [seducing] spirits and doctrines of demons.
—1 Timothy 4:1, nkjv

For such are false apostles, deceitful workers, transforming themselves into apostles of Christ. And no wonder! For Satan himself transforms himself into an angel of light. Therefore it is no great thing if his ministers also transform themselves into ministers of righteousness, whose end will be according to their works.
—2 Corinthians 11:13–15, nkjv

T HE DEVIL COULD sit on the front row in many church services throughout America today and never experience an uncomfortable moment. He is not disturbed by a message of cheap grace that gives believers a license to sin. Preaching that makes material prosperity the status symbol of faith doesn't upset him. A positive motivational message of love that has lost all its convictions doesn't even give him a mild case of indigestion. The seeker-sensitive gospel that is more concerned about making the unchurched feel comfortable than it is about convincing the lost that they need a Savior gives him a warm fuzzy feeling. Satan likes to listen to prophets who talk from their heads and then tag the utterance with "thus says the Lord." He is entertained by meetings where believers are so obsessed with manifestations they have no regard for order. He especially enjoys attending churches where grace is cheap and preachers choke on three-letter words like "sin."

In the absence of confrontation, men who manipulate and make merchandise of God's people become more arrogant and aggressive. The time has come for credible leaders to risk the repercussions of questioning some of the troubling trends of modern Christianity—even if it results in our being ostracized for daring to touch "God's anointed." False prophets won't go away unless they are forced to go away.

Seducing spirits have infected modern movements with doctrines of demons. They are behind the greed of the prosperity gospel, which has made material prosperity the status symbol of faith. They are behind the relevance sought by the seeker-sensitive movement, which restricts the moving of the Holy Spirit and leaves its adherents deficient in power to confront evil. They are behind the unhealthy obsession with the supernatural, which opens the door for manipulative leaders to grow rich by putting people on platforms or in front of TV cameras to tell stories that are often more paranormal than supernatural. They are behind the message of cheap grace, which gives those who love the pleasures of the world a license to sin. And they are on the other side of the street hiding behind legalism, which beats people to death for even entertaining a worldly thought. They are among the proud and insecure men who love titles and seek to impress others by giving titles to themselves. Jesus, John, Peter, and Paul warned us that they were coming. But many believers missed the memos. They think seducing spirits and false prophets are out there somewhere. But they are not just out *there*; they are in *here*. They are among us. They have found a home in several modern Charismatic movements.

Raising issues like these is not my favorite thing to do. I have no desire to be pugnacious. I love peace; but not the kind that comes through compromise with false prophets and evil spirits. A dislike for compromise has bought me a lot of undesired controversy. I once enjoyed material prosperity in a movement that was positive all the time. But when I began asking questions, I was accused of being negative. I have discovered through the years that preachers who operate deceitfully detest being called upon to answer questions—especially if they are asked in a public setting. False prophets don't attempt to hide their disdain for people who ask questions that force them to step out of the shadows into the light of truth.

Unfortunately, most deceivers are never called upon to answer questions. Seducing spirits have become comfortable, and doctrines of demons have become acceptable, among charismatics who don't question or confront anything out of fear that they will be accused of committing a horrible sin: touching "God's anointed." I knew that "God's anointed" would be upset by some of my questions but I asked them anyway—in spoken and written form. I asked them because I wasn't certain that some of their anointings came from God. And I asked them because I believed that famous leaders had conditioned the masses not to question them by misapplying and misusing several scriptures.

One of their favorite scriptures to misapply is 1 Chronicles 16:22: "Do not touch my anointed ones; do my prophets no harm." In that verse God spoke on behalf of His anointed. Authentic prophets didn't start parroting what God had said on their behalf everywhere they went; the false ones did. They twisted God's words and used them deceitfully to try to intimidate those who had the courage to question them.

Another verse often misapplied and misused in an attempt to intimidate critics is Matthew 7:1: "Do not judge, or you too will be judged." Deceptive leaders lift verses like this out of context, twist their meaning, and use them to their advantage. The New Testament has several verses that make it clear that we are to judge. The teaching of manipulative leaders who need a course in hermeneutics is certainly one of those things. Here are just a few verses which refute their false teaching on judgment:

> What business is it of mine to judge those outside the church? Are you not to judge those inside?
> —1 CORINTHIANS 5:12

> Or do you not know that the Lord's people will judge the world? And if you are to judge the world, are you not competent to judge trivial cases? Do you not know that we will judge angels? How much more the things of this life!
> —1 Corinthians 6:2–3

I am not shocked to find false prophets taking verses out of context and distorting their true meaning. What amazes me is that so many intelligent believers let them get away with it. It has to be the strong delusion Paul warned would come in the last days:

> The coming of the lawless one will be in accordance with how Satan works. He will use all sorts of displays of power through signs and wonders that serve the lie, and all the ways that wickedness deceives those who are perishing. They perish because they refused to love the truth and so be saved. For this reason God sends them a powerful delusion so that they will believe the lie.
> —2 Thessalonians 2:9–11

It is dangerous to distort, ignore, or play games with the truth: "For the wrath of God is revealed from heaven against all ungodliness and unrighteousness of men, who suppress the truth in unrighteousness" (Rom. 1:18, NKJV).

Seducing spirits use false apostles and prophets to pervert and distort the gospel. Sometimes they add to it and increase its demands; at other times they dilute it and diminish them. In the Charismatic movement today, the diluted version is most appealing. It places fewer requirements on those who embrace it. But it also makes them more vulnerable to deception. Is it possible that we are a bit deluded because we have, for too long, been willing to tolerate a tragic mixture of truth and error? Have we become so bereft of discernment that we are incapable of recognizing a self-promoting false prophet? Has our gospel been so diluted—have we so lowered the bar—that there is little distinguishable difference between those who call themselves Christians and those who do not?

Dilution is dangerous. The *Merriam-Webster Online* dictionary gives this definition of *dilute*: "to make [something] thinner or weaker by adding water or another liquid; to lessen the strength [or effect] of (something)."[1] Is the modern gospel weaker than the one preached in the Book of Acts? Has it lost some of its strength and effect? A thinking person is compelled to wonder if the failure of the modern church in America to impact the culture is not directly connected to the dilution of the gospel. Should not those who realize this return to the gospel of power preached by the first Christians?

We need to think—really think—about what is happening in the church today. Deceiving spirits, doctrines of demons, false apostles, deceitful workers, Satan transforming himself into an angel of light and pretending to be one of the good guys: it is scary stuff—stuff a lot of Christians don't even want to hear about, much less think about. They prefer to live with the idea that false prophets and seducing spirits are out there somewhere, but certainly not in the neighborhood. The truth is: they are not just *around* us but *among* us. They have become comfortable in churches that dilute or distort the gospel.

We must pray and think clearly in order to recognize

the work of deceiving spirits among us. We must add diligent study to our praying and thinking in order to deal with the doctrines of demons that have corrupted our theology. And we must ask questions that are designed to make others think. If we don't come out of the fog soon, a growing army of self-appointed extrabiblical apostles and prophets is going to drive us all into the ditch. Peter warned us to "be alert and of sober mind. Your enemy the devil prowls around like a roaring lion looking for someone to devour" (1 Pet. 5:8).

Seducing spirits contaminate the atmospheres they invade. Much of the modern church has inhaled the impure air of contaminated Christianity for so long it has forgotten what it is like to breathe the pure oxygen of the Holy Spirit. The contamination has clouded our discernment. A tragic mixture of truth and error has confused us. Surveys reveal that the modern church is not well grounded in the Word of God. Sound doctrine has taken a back seat to exciting experiences and entertaining services. We have been confused by too many voices—too much information (much of it false) from too many different sources. The confusion has caused us to stumble around in a spiritual haze that clouds our discernment and dulls our senses. We need to spend more time in the Bible, listening for the voice of the Spirit—and more time doing the hard work of thinking.

Confusion over what we believe always leaves the door open to dangerous delusions. Is it possible that many modern Christians are victims of delusion without realizing it? Lack of sound doctrine and failure to think clearly tip the scales in favor of delusion. Is that why so few even consider the possibility that the false prophets Jesus and the apostles warned us to be looking for in the last days are already here? False prophets seldom look or act like we expect them to. The truth is, they have been with us since the days of the early church and there are more of them today than ever before. Jesus warned that they would be everywhere in the last days. So, where are they? If you believe what Jesus said, and what the apostles wrote, it should not surprise you to hear me assert that they are both out *there* and in *here*. They are among us. They are preaching in our pulpits, on Christian television and radio, on the Internet, and every other form of media imaginable. The problem is not just that they are preaching but that so many believe and practice what they are preaching—even when it costs a lot to do so. It must be the result of strong delusion.

Delusion is dangerous but the deluded seem to love their delusions. They tend to hold tightly to them in spite of credible evidence that contradicts them. I said earlier that the Apostle Paul warned in 2 Thessalonians 2:10–11 that strong delusion comes to those who believe a lie because they do not love the truth. I didn't want to think that some who profess Christ are delusional. But I don't think there is another explanation. I became convinced delusion was in the air when I showed people solid evidence—numerous scriptures—that contradicted what they purported to believe; they were unmoved. Several agreed that the scriptures did not support their beliefs, but they rejected the scriptures and held on to the doctrines of their favorite false prophets anyway. That is the delusion

Paul warned would come in the last days—a delusion delivered by seducing spirits and doctrines of demons.

False prophets are not financed by the world but by Christians who are deceived by them. Supporting a false prophet who leads you astray is akin to paying for medicine that is making you sick. People do it all the time because they are not careful. They don't read the labels and don't take time to think about dangerous side effects or the interactions of new medications with ones already being taken. They trust the instructions of doctors who may not be as informed as they should be about the patient or the drug or may be unduly influenced by a drug company or their salesman. People who don't ask questions are not thinking as carefully or as clearly as they should be. What they thought was helping is actually harming them. When the light comes on, they sometimes ask, "Why would the doctor give me medication that harms me?" The answer is not always a simple one. Sometimes it's because he is not thinking either.

During a long battle with malaria, I did a lot of research. It didn't take me long to realize that I was more informed about various medicines and their side effects than most of my doctors. As I struggled to recover, I was pressured to take medications which I refused to take. One doctor threatened to declare me noncompliant, which would have affected my insurance coverage, because I refused a medication that I knew to be dangerous. I held my ground and finally got to a brilliant neurologist and infectious disease doctor who were cautious with prescriptions—especially to someone like me whose problems were not only from malaria but from a reaction to Lariam (Mefloquine) prescribed to treat it, which caused serious central nervous system damage. The medicine hurt me more than the mosquito that gave me malaria! I started reading and thinking more diligently and asking a lot more questions about doctors and the medications they prescribed. I seriously doubt that I would be writing books or preaching today had I not asked so many questions and declined nearly every medication suggested other than antibiotics. I chose to rely more on prayer, vitamins, and exercise.

I advise people to treat prophets and preachers like I did doctors. Thinking, asking questions, and exercising discernment can save you a lot of grief. It is ludicrous to receive a prophecy from someone you don't know, or don't know well, without carefully determining if it lines up with Scripture. We need to be more like the Bereans who searched the scriptures daily and diligently to make sure preachers were telling them the truth. They even questioned and carefully examined the teachings of the Apostle Paul: "Now the Berean Jews were of more noble character than those in Thessalonica, for they received the message with great eagerness and examined the Scriptures every day to see if what Paul said was true" (Acts 17:11). Much of the confusion in the Charismatic movement would come to an end, and a lot of false prophets and self-appointed apostles would be put out of business, if we followed the example of the Berean Jews.

The man-made empires of seducers in the modern church have been constructed with generous offerings and purchases of books, CDs, and countless other products by Christians who aren't thinking or carefully reading the labels. Ingenuous supporters never think of their favorite dispensers of "spiritual medicine" as false prophets. How could they be? They seem nice and their teachings are often positive and encouraging. But there is often poison in the pill. A little Berean-style examination would detect it.

Few charismatic believers have thought seriously about what I call the "tragic mixture." Deception often comes wrapped in truth. I am careful about what I drink when I am in foreign countries with people I don't know. I have been with people who seemed awfully nice but, upon closer scrutiny and examination, I discovered that some were nothing more than a demon with skin stretched over it. I don't drink poison simply because the nice person dispensing it has a charming smile. A cup of coffee may taste great, even if it comes laced with a drop of strychnine. It may be 99 percent coffee; but if you drink it you will be seriously sick or seriously dead. The same is true with false doctrine.

If you were the devil, how would you deceive people? Probably by mixing error with truth. If you could ask Eve, she would tell you that a lot of trouble can come from something that sounds great, looks beautiful, and tastes sweet. That is the way of seduction. It will make you think that something that is harming you is the greatest thing since sliced bread.

The church in America is losing ground in both numbers and influence. Church growth is not keeping pace with the growth of the population. We have more churches, more Christian organizations, and more television and radio preachers than any other nation; but, with all its resources, the American church becomes less effective day by day. Never has a church accomplished so little with so much. Doctrines of demons, propagated by some of the most famous and most popular preachers in America, have produced an anemic church that has lost the power to impact culture.

In the pages that follow, I launch an in-your-face affront to the deceivers who have infiltrated the modern church; and I make an appeal to their victims. The material is sometimes presented in a confrontational manner in order to provoke serious thought. My prayer is that it will inspire those who are looking for the Light to pray for discernment—discernment that will enable us to recognize the impostors. Ultimately, it is offered in the hope that truth will open the eyes of all who decide to diligently study the Word of God and depend on the Holy Spirit. I pray that, after reading these pages, you will join the growing number of sincere believers who dare to touch "God's anointed" and try the spirits: "Dear friends, don't believe all people who say that they have the Spirit. Instead, test them. See whether the spirit they have is from God, because there are many false prophets in the world" (1 John 4:1, GW). It is crucial that we begin to exercise our senses to discern between good and evil (Heb. 5:14).

I was honored to work with B. H. Clendennen, one of the true Pentecostal pioneers of the last century. He founded the School of Christ International which spread to over one hundred nations. In an earlier book I shared a discussion Brother Clendennen had while in China. Between sessions of the school there, he met often with key leaders in the underground church who shared their thoughts about the church in America. They were aware of the prosperity gospel and the tendency of American Christians to pursue the "good life." They laughed about the American dream and wondered how Christians on their way to heaven could become so obsessed with the material world. Clendennen spoke several times about a renowned Chinese leader who visited the USA at the invitation of Christian leaders here. His hosts took him to visit megachurches, universities, and large ministries. As he prepared to return to China, one of the American leaders asked him what most impressed him about the church in the USA. He was not impressed at all; he told them that he was most impressed by how much the church in America had been able to accomplish without the help of the Holy Spirit.[2]

What an indictment! That humble Chinese leader summed up with just a few words why much of the American church has lost power and influence—without the help of the Holy Spirit. Some churches won't even allow Him to administer His gifts in meetings. Did you ever think about how audacious it is for a puny human to tell the omnipotent Spirit of God that He is not allowed to move in a meeting? God has been displaced and man is at the center. We still call it Christianity, but sometimes it looks like a mere form of powerless humanism wearing a religious face. The Holy Spirit likes authenticity. He can be grieved to the point of withdrawing from churches and ministries that do not possess it. The sad thing is that so few even realize He is gone. Church services go on week after week but only a few notice that something is missing. Even fewer are willing to admit that God no longer attends their services. That is what eventually happens when people tolerate, or even welcome, a form of godliness that has lost all its power (2 Tim. 3:5). Seducing spirits move in to fill the void left by the absence of the Holy Spirit. The devil sits on the front row through the entire service and never experiences an uncomfortable moment. People don't even recognize him. He feels right at home in an atmosphere emptied of conviction and the power of the Spirit.

The life of God has left churches that were once filled with excitement and expectation. The Holy Spirit withdrew from churches where He was no longer wanted; and leaders who entertained seducing spirits and doctrines of demons did not protest His departure. They chose to give themselves to all manner of frivolous fleshly activity rather than yield to His holy presence. Grieved, He went weeping away and seducing spirits came to take His place. Sadly, few even noticed His exit. God doesn't like mixture. He will not share His glory with another (Isa. 42:8; 48:11). When egotistical leaders choose to glory in the flesh and take control of meetings, and when people love to have it so, He will withdraw. He will not remain in an atmosphere of disorder where unrestrained flesh and emotion rule and the foul influence of unclean spirits contaminates the atmosphere. Nor will He remain where there is order, if leaders restrict His movement.

The Holy Spirit gives discernment and places checks in our spirits. But if leaders ignore His warnings and give false prophets a license to operate freely, He will withdraw to search for lovers of truth who yet desire to "contend for the faith which was once delivered unto the saints" (Jude 1:20, KJV). When believers sacrifice truth in the pursuit of exhilarating experience, they are in essence refusing to yield to the presence of the Holy One. The Spirit loves excitement, but He loathes the chaos and confusion that prevail in the absence or neglect of truth. He doesn't like an atmosphere of levity created by leaders who subjugate truth to experience.

> Yet a time is coming and has now come when the true worshipers will worship the Father in the Spirit and in truth, for they are the kind of worshipers the Father seeks. God is spirit, and his worshipers must worship in the Spirit and in truth.
> —John 4:23–24

These are tough times for godly pastors. A sincere pastor who discerns what is happening is often discouraged in his attempts to correct the problem. He finds it nearly impossible to compete with all the big preachers on Christian television. Many of his members have their favorites and listen to them for several hours every week. The pastor has no more than an hour on Sunday and maybe forty-five minutes during the midweek service. Believers become confused listening to so many different voices—especially when much of what they hear caters to the flesh and its desires. The Bible truth preached by sincere pastors sounds like a foreign language to those who are drunk on the wine of false prophets, and may evoke a strong reaction from some of his members. It is a difficult time for faithful pastors who are committed to preach the whole counsel of God.

The prosperity-preaching, seed-seeking televangelists are just the tip of the iceberg. The modern church is filled with teachings and philosophies of ministry that have little or no scriptural foundation. The seeker-sensitive philosophy of ministry has sacrificed power on the altars of relevance. In the seeker-sensitive world, casual dialed-down Christianity has displaced the dynamic dialed-up variety of the New Testament. I am compelled to wonder: What good is relevance without power?

Some of the preachers who claim to have power are laughed at by non-Christians who recognize con men sooner than most Christians. They only tune in to Christian television for entertainment. To them, it is great comedy. They laugh at faith and prosperity preachers, false prophets, self-appointed apostles, and cons masquerading as men of God. They really get a kick out of the seed-seekers who constantly come up with new gimmicks to extract money from the gullible. And you probably know this: During the holy laughter movement and the Toronto Blessing they weren't laughing with us; they were laughing at us. Most non-Christians are not seduced by the pretenders. They seem to have more discernment than naive Christians who bury pleasure loving preachers in their hard-earned money.

The only hope for the modern church is to get back to the Bible and to the passion and power of Pentecost. To reach this generation, we must honestly face our impotence and cry out for a fresh baptism of the Holy Spirit. Nothing short of authentic revival that restores the credibility of the church can impact our culture or save our nation. Sincere believers must take action necessary for recovery. I question the effectiveness of Christianity that conforms to the culture in a futile attempt to be relevant and gain acceptance rather than confronting it and producing change. Pastors who have made peace with powerless Christianity should be indicted for ministerial malpractice. We don't need churches or leaders who are more concerned with creating a comfortable non-offensive atmosphere for the unchurched than about seriously endeavoring to carry out the Great Commission. We don't need more seed-seekers and greedy faith preachers. We don't need more self-appointed apostles and prophets. We need leaders with character who love truth and preach the whole counsel of God in the power of the Spirit.

The time has come for godly leaders to raise honest questions about several of the misrepresentations of New Testament Christianity that plague our nation today. We should not be hesitant to challenge the credibility of polite religion that is reluctant to question anything out of fear of touching "God's anointed." I fear that this casual non-confrontational Christianity, with such shallow commitment and almost no conviction, won't survive the coming storm. Halfhearted Christians will be devoured by a wholehearted devil.

Much of the modern church is not willing to confront anything. It fails to understand the difference between acceptance and tolerance. Some believers have elevated political correctness over Bible truth; others have subjugated truth to experience. Those who esteem truth know that while we may be required to tolerate things we don't agree with, it is not wise to accept them. Accepting what the Bible condemns is a sure formula for disaster. The destruction of Sodom and Gomorrah vividly reveals what is at the end of that road. Lukewarm believers have embraced a watered-down kind of love that has lost all its convictions. Reverence and the fear of God are seldom even mentioned from many pulpits today (Heb. 12:28).

We are in great danger and few even realize it. God will be forced to judge a compromised, contaminated church which exalts political correctness over Bible truth. Warnings have become rare. When lightweight prophets sheepishly give them, they always take the edge off by adding a positive promise. We need a wakeup call from a heavyweight like Elijah, Jeremiah, or John the Baptist. Few Christians fully perceive the danger of the times we are living in.

> But as the days of Noah were, so also will the coming of the Son of Man be. For as in the days before the flood, they were eating and drinking, marrying and giving in marriage, until the day that Noah entered the ark, and did not know until the flood came and took them all away, so also will the coming of the Son of Man be.
> —MATTHEW 24:37–39, NKJV

What was it like in the days of Noah? Evil spread like a pervasive plague over the whole earth. But even in the face of increasing darkness, people ignored the warnings. They went on with business as usual not realizing that destruction was at the door. Can you imagine how they felt when the door was shut and they realized it was too late?

Beliefs and philosophies of ministry that are undermining authentic Christianity must be assailed by those who have some sense of what is coming. Leaders must put on strength and earnestly contend for the faith. Those who are liberal in their application and careless in their handling of the Word of God must no longer be given a pass. The deception of leaders who deliberately violate basic rules of hermeneutics in order to distort the clear meaning of scripture that refutes their favorite teachings must be exposed. Those who create error and imbalance by emphasizing one truth to the neglect of others must be confronted. Those who see the corruption of the modern church must lift their voices to cry out for repentance and a return to the credible Christianity of the Book of Acts.

I hope to stir the hearts of believers who long for real revival and convict the hearts of those who don't. Doing so demands the slaughter of several sacred cows. I plan to assault everything from an aberrant gospel of love that has lost all its convictions, to grace that excuses sin, to the delusion that has made material prosperity the status symbol of faith. I plan to expose the covetousness of seed-seekers and the craftiness of con men masquerading as preachers on Christian television. It is my prayer that truth will once again rule the minds and resonate in the hearts of believers who yet long for authentic Christianity. I urge those who have had enough of polite, politically correct religion to find the strength to stand against it. Elijah and Jeremiah did. They were greatly outnumbered, but history clearly shows that God was with the minority. Nobody knows the names of the false prophets they confronted, but untold millions still remember the names of Elijah and Jeremiah.

Stephen and the Apostle Paul didn't let diabolic attacks from an army of false prophets shut them up. Nobody remembers the names of the Pharisees who stoned Stephen or those of the legalists and liberals who dogged the trail of the great apostle. But untold millions throughout the world are well acquainted with both Stephen and Paul. Two thousand years down the road from their martyrdom we are still quoting their teachings and naming our children after them.

We must seek inspiration from the great men and women of faith who throughout history have stood for truth and refused compromise. Their sacrifice for the love of the truth, and their boldness to confront the false, should infuse us with boldness to rise up and confront the darkness that so often goes unchallenged in the modern church.

Chapter 2

SPIRITUAL SPECIALISTS

Spiritual specialists are springing up like mushrooms in a manure pile after a warm rain. They are often not only extrabiblical or unbiblical, but selectively biblical. That is, they are biblical when it suits them to be. The faith specialists were the first in the modern church to hang out their shingles, but many others have followed. Today we have an abundance of love specialists and grace specialists and prophecy specialists, and too many more to mention. Since the faith guys were the first ones out of the gate, I am giving them more attention up front; I will get to some of the newer kids on the block later.

I preach both faith and prosperity. I believe that it is important for Christians to maintain a positive confession of faith. The Bible leaves no doubt that God wants His people to exercise faith to receive His help and blessing. The Apostle John told his spiritual children, "Beloved, I pray that you may prosper in all things and be in health, just as your soul prospers" (3 John 1:2, NKJV). No one who reads the Bible should have an argument with real faith and true prosperity. However, we should note that John's idea of prosperity, or that of Jesus and all the apostles, was much different than that of prosperity preachers today. You only have to read the verses the word of faith preachers won't read to know that something is wrong with their doctrine. The problem with word of faith preachers is not just what they preach; it is what they don't preach. They deliberately emphasize only a select portion of scripture—all positive. Somehow, word of faith preachers get away with deliberately leaving out what they don't like. That is a serious preacher crime. Those who commit it should be put on trial for ministerial malpractice.

How can they call themselves "word" preachers and omit so much of the Word? Why do they deliberately leave out so much scripture? They do it because the scriptures they omit contradict what they have chosen to believe and teach. They don't want to be corrected or adjusted by the Word of God. Their insistence on the right to specialize, and arbitrarily select only their favorite positive passages, should alert us to the danger of what they are doing. If that is not enough, the fact that they keep parroting the same things over and over should wake us up. I know they have conditioned us to believe it is wrong to touch "God's anointed," but has it ever dawned on you that they may be misapplying that scripture too?

I believe that not only do we have the right to question whether proponents of the modern faith and prosperity gospel are operating in the authentic faith of the Bible—we have the responsibility. Real faith looks like Jesus and His apostles: It talks like them, acts like them, lives like them. We need to examine the message and lifestyle of modern leaders by comparing them to Jesus and the apostles and to the message of faith they preached. If what they preach or the way they live does not line up with scripture, they should be willing to make corrections and adjustments, shouldn't they?

I am on board with the faith and prosperity outlined in the Bible. However, I take issue with the modern faith and prosperity gospel. I believe it is a perverted misrepresentation of the authentic message of faith. Modern proponents of the faith and prosperity gospel often call themselves "word" preachers. It seems reasonable to assume that someone calling himself a word preacher should be willing to be corrected or adjusted by the Word; but I know from personal experience they most often are not. Many "word" preachers I have dealt with, especially in America, don't handle the Word with the integrity they claim. I have dealt with several who do not follow, and some who don't even know, the basic rules of hermeneutics.[1]

Most word of faith preachers don't approach the Bible to be instructed, corrected, or adjusted. They approach it searching for more support for what they have already chosen to believe. In fact, many "word" preachers don't even spend much time in the Word. That is why their sermons are filled with stories, testimonies, "shucking and jiving," and not much real Bible preaching. The ones lower down the food chain spend more time reading books and watching and listening to the big boys who are a level or two or three above them. The lowly "wannabes" have been taught that the only way to the next level is by listening to and learning from those who are higher up the ladder than you, and by sowing seed upward into the level to which you want to rise. If you give enough, you might be invited to fly with them on one of their jets to a meeting somewhere. You might even get to stay with them in one of the hotels that few of the common folk even know exist—the ones with rooms that cost several hundred and even thousands of dollars a night.

If you keep sowing good seeds into the level above, you might eventually find yourself on a platform somewhere with one of the big boys. Play by the rules long enough and you might be admitted as a junior member into their prestigious club. Get enough attention, gather enough followers, accumulate enough money, and you might evolve to a higher level on the food chain. But be forewarned: You won't hear them saying what Zig Ziglar used to say everywhere he spoke: "See you at the top." You won't hear it because there isn't much room at the top in the word of faith world; and the room that is left is guarded very carefully. This is a very exclusive club.

If you are a word of faith preacher, you might want to pause to think about this: Do you really want to keep sowing your seed upward in the hope of being allowed entrance into the next level someday? Maybe it would be better to hang out with Jesus down here among the common people who hear Him gladly (Mark 12:37, NKJV). The faith of Jesus took Him lower before it took Him higher. He didn't expend any effort or thought trying to figure out how to climb up higher. He humbled Himself and trusted God to raise Him up. Does this sound like a different gospel? Not to those who read—really read—the Bible.

> Let this mind be in you which was also in Christ Jesus, who, being in the form of God, did not consider it robbery to be equal with God, but made Himself of no reputation, taking the form of a bondservant, and coming in the likeness of men. And being found in appearance as a man He humbled Himself and became obedient to the point of death, even the death of the cross. Therefore God has highly exalted Him and given Him the name which is above every name, that at the name of Jesus every knee should bow…and that every tongue should confess that Jesus Christ is Lord, to the glory of God the Father.
> —Philippians 2:5–11, nkjv

Have you been trying to sow your way up to the next level? Jesus didn't do it that way. He didn't instruct His disciples to try to do it that way. Striving to go higher might eventually land you lower. The devil knows that better than any of us. He is abased because of pride that strived to climb higher. Jesus is exalted because of humility that made Him willing to go lower. According to the Bible, the way up is down: "Humble yourself in the sight of the Lord, and He will lift you up" (James 4:10, nkjv).

> But Jesus called them to Himself and said, "You know that the rulers of the Gentiles lord it over them, and those who are great exercise authority over them. Yet it shall not be so among you, but whoever desires to become great among you, let him be your servant. And whoever desires to be first among you, let him be your slave—just as the Son of

Man did not come to be served, but to serve, and to give His life a ransom for many."
—Matthew 20:25–28

When is the last time you heard a word of faith preacher preach about going low, humbling yourself, and becoming a servant? Those verses don't mesh well with teachings on wealth, dominion, and living like a king's kid. I have discovered that word of faith preachers avoid passages that contradict what they have chosen to believe. Convenient isn't it? They treat the Bible like a buffet where you get to choose what you want to eat. "Give me some faith and prosperity. I will take a double portion of love and joy. Hold up man: I don't want any of that humility and service. I'm going to pass on the commitment and conviction. What's that? Suffering and sacrifice: I don't even believe in it." Do we really have the right to pick what we want and pass on the rest? Today we have faith specialists, love specialists, grace specialists, etc., *ad nauseam*. Does a preacher who is truly called by God into the ministry have the right to be a spiritual specialist who only preaches on positive subjects, or does the Holy Spirit move real preachers to proclaim the whole counsel of God?

Word of faith preachers wouldn't deliberately avoid passages that contradict their chosen belief system, would they? Here is a good example of them being selectively biblical: deliberately avoiding or leaving out what they don't want to face. They regularly preach on the positive section of Hebrews 11—you know the chapter that begins with, "Now faith is the substance of things hoped for, the evidence of things not seen…" (Heb. 11:1, NKJV). I bet you have heard even more references to verse 6, "But without faith it is impossible to please Him, for he who comes to God must believe that He is, and that He is a rewarder of those who diligently seek Him" (NKJV).

You would expect word of faith preachers to quote these verses often. After all, this chapter is often called "Faith's Hall of Fame." But how many sermons have you heard on the last part of the chapter? I wonder why so many avoid it altogether or try to explain it away? Why would any sincere "word" preacher choose to deliberately ignore or avoid any portion of the Bible? Why would he read a passage that needs no interpretation and then say, "This isn't really what it means?" Or even worse (and I have personally heard this said), "If those saints would have had the full revelation of faith that we do, they wouldn't have had to suffer like that." Why would anyone follow a preacher who handled the Word of God with so little integrity? All scripture is profitable and inspired by the Holy Spirit, isn't it? The Apostle Paul thought so (2 Tim. 3:16). Could it be simply that word of faith preachers avoid it because all the suffering, lack, and persecution in the last part of Hebrews 11 doesn't support their chosen belief system? Does it demonstrate godly character to grab what the Bible says on health and wealth and throw away what it says on sacrifice and suffering?

The first twenty-three verses are all victory, and word of faith preachers love them. But they start having trouble with Moses in verse 24. They just can't get their materialistic minds wrapped around how Moses could have "refused to be known as the son of Pharaoh's daughter." Their love for the "good life" makes it impossible for them to understand why the great leader turned his back on all the pleasures of Egypt: "He chose to be mistreated along with the people of God rather than to enjoy the fleeting pleasures of sin" (v. 25). If saying no to pleasure was not enough, Moses turned his back on a whole lot of treasure too. No wonder they won't honestly preach these verses: "He regarded disgrace for the sake of Christ as of greater value than the treasures of Egypt..." (v. 26). They simply cannot understand how Moses, positioned as he was for power, prestige, and prosperity, could forsake it all and go live as a nomadic shepherd. But that is just what he did. I like the way the KJV says it: "By faith he forsook Egypt, not fearing the wrath of the king: for he endured, as seeing him who is invisible" (v. 27). They don't understand why he did it. But I do—his heart was set on a different kingdom. What Moses valued most was spiritual, not material.

I wouldn't preach those verses either if I were a word of faith preacher. They demolish the foundation of the whole faith and prosperity movement. Those verses scare them so badly they don't even try to twist them like they do so many others—they avoid them altogether. They may be foolish enough to trade spiritual treasures for material ones, but they are not crazy enough to touch those verses. The KJV says that Moses chose "to suffer affliction with the people of God" (v. 25). They disagree with the Word they claim to preach. They don't even believe that suffering or affliction could ever be the will of God. They certainly aren't going to choose it. Thinker alert! Moses rejected what word of faith preachers have chosen. He trashed what they esteem so highly. He refused what they lust for. He forsook what they covet. No wonder they are "selectively" biblical.

If Jesus had believed and lived by word of faith doctrines, He never would have left the great treasures of heaven to come to earth. He certainly would not have been born in a stable. He would not have lived a life of sacrifice and suffering among people who rejected Him. There is no way He would have spent so much time with the poor and oppressed. In short, if Jesus had been word of faith, we would have no Savior. Satan would be our master and we would still be dead in trespasses and sins.

The way Jesus and Moses lived is a rebuke to preachers and followers of word of faith teaching. "Faith's Hall of Fame" hits prosperity preachers right between the eyes. Two words in the middle of verse 35 send them running for cover—"and others." The "others" suffered deprivation, persecution, and even martyrdom; yet God commends them for their faith and lists them with those who did great exploits. If I were a word of faith preacher, I would stop right there at "and others" to repent and ask God to deliver me from false teaching. They love to talk about all the great exploits, great successes, miraculous events, dead people raised, etc., from verse 28 to verse 35. It is exciting reading and it fits right into their perverted selectively biblical approach.

But right in the middle of verse 35 everything changes. They try hard to avoid reading the verses in the last part of Hebrews 11, much less saying them out loud. I have watched some of the less calloused ones get confused to the point of stuttering trying to explain them. Portions of the Word that say things like "and others were tortured, not accepting deliverance" don't agree with the "word" they preach—so they just leave it out. The error of word of faith preachers is not just what they preach—it's what they don't preach.

Let's read more of these verses from the Word that "word" preachers run from:

> And others had trial of cruel mockings and scourgings, yea, moreover of bonds and imprisonment: They were stoned, they were sawn asunder, were tempted, were slain with the sword: they wandered about in sheepskins and goatskins; being destitute, afflicted, tormented; (Of whom the world was not worthy:) they wandered in deserts, and in mountains, and in dens and caves of the earth. And these all, having obtained a good report through faith, received not the promise.
> —HEBREWS 11:36–39, KJV

This is the true Bible message of faith—it takes the positive and the negative. It does not attempt to avoid or explain away persecution and suffering. It doesn't deny them or try to confess them out of reality. It faces them confidently and emerges from them victoriously. Who but a deceiver, or the deceived, would run from such clear accounts in the Bible? Let's respond to these verses like we are people who believe that "all scripture is profitable." Let's honor these victorious sufferers who were commended by God for their faith. If God commended them, shouldn't we? You have to be deficient in your thinking to distort passages like this or to avoid them because they mess with your doctrine. You have to be more than messed up to belittle these great heroes and suggest that some flaw in their faith caused their suffering. God clearly commends these sufferers for their great faith.

Why would people who suffered so much love God so deeply? In the face of lack, suffering, and severe persecution, how did they hold on to faith and hope? The answer is simple: Their faith was not looking for the good life in this world. They knew that heaven was at the end of the road. Like Moses, they chose to suffer affliction with the people of God rather than to enjoy the passing pleasures of sin (Heb. 11:25). They were after something eternal, and no amount of difficulty or sacrifice in this world deterred them from their search. Like Abraham, they were looking for an eternal "city with foundations, whose architect and builder is God" (v. 10). The modern faith and prosperity gospel totally rejects such ideas of suffering and persecution, even though they are clearly established in the Bible. Isn't being so "selectively" biblical a bit heretical?

Word of faith preachers work hard to avoid such passages and even harder to avoid having to answer questions about them. If you want to hear some foolish answers, do what I have done at times: politely ask a word of faith preacher during a group conversation, perhaps when you are eating steak or lobster with them at a nice restaurant after a meeting, to explain Hebrews 11:35–39. Chances are you won't be invited to go out with them after a meeting again. Count the cost before putting them in a position to defend their "selectively" biblical ways. But if you love the truth more than steak or lobster, go ahead and do it. It makes for interesting conversation. When challenged to honestly face scriptures like these, they often attempt to dismiss them or offer a feeble counter to them—usually some overused verse from the blessing and victory side of faith. They demonstrate no regard for basic rules of hermeneutics which insist that doctrine be formulated by taking the clear message of the Bible at face value and by comparing scripture with scripture in order to properly interpret and apply it. Sadly, most people let them get away with it. If you become one of the ones who doesn't, you will soon realize that some of them need less teaching on faith and more on the fruit of the Spirit.

They wouldn't deliberately violate the rules of hermeneutics and twist scripture to make it conform to the lavish lifestyles they have chosen, would they? They wouldn't subjugate scripture to their own desires, would they? That would demonstrate a serious lack of character and integrity, wouldn't it? I think you know the answers. Let's look at a specific example that has to do with the issue of suffering. Word of faith leaders flatly deny that it could ever be the will of God for a believer to suffer. If you doubt my assertion, just Google something like "word of faith doctrine on suffering." But don't try to read it all. You would never get back to this book.

The Bible says exactly the opposite of what "word" preachers say. "But even if you should suffer for righteousness' sake, *you are* blessed. And do not be afraid of their threats, nor be troubled" (1 Pet. 3:14, NKJV). Peter certainly disagrees with modern word of faith teaching. He goes so far as to say that you are blessed when you "suffer for righteousness' sake." Paul would trash their teaching too. He actually prayed for the privilege of entering into the sufferings of Jesus. Word of faith preachers will tell you that he was just speaking of suffering in the spiritual sense; but all you have to do is look at his life to dispense with that erroneous idea. It is just one of many of their distorted views that can be easily refuted with scripture.

Paul told Timothy that "all who desire to live godly in Christ Jesus will suffer persecution" (2 Tim. 3:12). That should answer all the questions. Paul uses "suffer" and "persecution" in the same short verse and declares that both are a result of godliness. It should lead one to ask, "If word of faith preachers never suffer, what kind of lives are they living?" If Paul is right, and I suspect that he is, they are evidently not living godly ones. A lot of godly people are suffering today, and it is not due to a lack of faith. We should not stand silently by and let faith preachers make people who suffer think that their faith is deficient.

Let's briefly look at the issue of suffering and the will of God. Faith teachers have from the earliest days of the movement said the same thing that people like Mary Baker Eddy and the positive mind science groups have said since the 1800s: all suffering is mental or spiritual and it can be corrected by right thinking and believing. In fact, a lot of word of faith doctrine sounds exactly like the teachings of Christian Science (space won't allow me to follow that trail farther here, but I do in an upcoming book entitled *Of Money and Men*).

Anyone who has listened to or read the books of word of faith preachers knows that they often say that it is not God's will for a Christian to suffer—not ever. But what does the Bible say? "So then, those who suffer according to God's will should commit themselves to their faithful Creator and continue to do good" (1 Pet. 4:19). That verse and many others contradict one of the favorite teachings of the Word of Faith movement. They claim to be "word" preachers, but they deliberately avoid or even ignore the Word when it contradicts the doctrine they have developed—a doctrine that supports their unscriptural lifestyles. Shouldn't more of us be politely saying, "False doctrine"; or maybe boldly asking, "Is this heresy?" I want to take a little time here to illustrate how far off the tracks the word of faith preachers really are in this area (and it is just one of many areas that could be addressed). I will share several scriptures and refrain from comment. The scriptures speak well enough for themselves. This lengthy list of scriptures contains just a few of many on the subject. They clearly show how willing these men are to blatantly violate scripture and to brazenly teach doctrines contrary to it.

> I will show him how much he must suffer for my name.
> —Acts 9:16

> Not only so, but we also glory in our sufferings, because we know that suffering produces perseverance.
> —Romans 5:3

> I ask you, therefore, not to be discouraged because of my sufferings for you, which are your glory.
> —Ephesians 3:13

> For it has been granted to you on behalf of Christ not only to believe in him, but also to suffer for him.
> —Philippians 1:29

Now I rejoice in what I am suffering for you, and I fill up in my flesh what is still lacking in regard to Christ's afflictions, for the sake of his body, which is the church.
—Colossians 1:24

You became imitators of us and of the Lord, for you welcomed the message in the midst of severe suffering with the joy given by the Holy Spirit.
—1 Thessalonians 1:6

So do not be ashamed of the testimony about our Lord or of me his prisoner. Rather, join with me in suffering for the gospel, by the power of God.
—2 Timothy 1:8

Join with me in suffering, like a good soldier of Christ Jesus.
—2 Timothy 2:3

This is my gospel, for which I am suffering even to the point of being chained like a criminal. But God's word is not chained.
—2 Timothy 2:8–9

In all this you greatly rejoice, though now for a little while you may have had to suffer grief in all kinds of trials.
—1 Peter 1:6

For it is commendable if someone bears up under the pain of unjust suffering because they are conscious of God. But how is it to your credit if you receive a beating for doing wrong and endure it? But if you suffer for doing good and you endure it, this is commendable before God. To this you were

called, because Christ suffered for you, leaving you an example, that you should follow in his steps.
—1 Peter 2:19–21

Therefore, since Christ suffered in his body, arm yourselves also with the same attitude, because whoever suffers in the body is done with sin.
—1 Peter 4:1

But rejoice inasmuch as you participate in the sufferings of Christ, so that you may be overjoyed when his glory is revealed.
—1 Peter 4:13

However, if you suffer as a Christian, do not be ashamed, but praise God that you bear that name.
—1 Peter 4:16

Resist him, standing firm in the faith, because you know that the family of believers throughout the world is undergoing the same kind of sufferings. And the God of all grace, who called you to his eternal glory in Christ, after you have suffered a little while, will himself restore you and make you strong, firm and steadfast.
—1 Peter 5:9–10

I shared all of the preceding scriptures, which are just a few of many on the well established doctrine of suffering in the Bible, to make a point. Word of faith preachers unabashedly violate hermeneutics and deliberately take scriptures out of context to distort their true meanings. They ignore them altogether if they disprove their false doctrine. This is among the brashest, most blatant acts of disrespect for the authority of the Word of God I have ever witnessed. It is deplorable that anyone who calls himself a "word" preacher could show such glaring disregard for the Bible. It is impossible for me to believe that leaders could ignore such a large body of truth without doing so deliberately. How have they gotten away with it for so long? It must be a strong delusion that results from the deception of seducing spirits.

It demonstrates a serious lack of integrity to dismiss scriptures because they challenge and contradict your belief system. A sincere believer is always teachable and willing to be corrected by Scripture. Followers of word of faith preachers should seriously question the character of leaders who deliberately leave huge segments of scripture out of their messages. These leaders know that most people prefer a message of prosperity and victory over one that includes persecution or suffering. But even a shred of integrity in handling Scripture should prevent them from rejecting or deliberately trying to distort the meaning of passages which call their doctrine into question. We must approach the Word of God with the kind of reverence that causes us to bow to its authority. We must be willing to have it correct us and adjust our doctrine. The refusal of modern faith preachers to honestly present the whole counsel of God—positive and negative—should cause every thinking Christian to question their aberrant theology.

Hebrews 11:35-40 presents true Bible faith that is endorsed by God Himself. It is faith that stands in the face of persecution, suffering, and lack. It is faith that does not run from or deny suffering but rises victoriously out of it. It is faith that lays down its life as a martyr—not questioning, but feeling honored to be allowed the privilege of sacrificing for the gospel's sake. It is real Bible faith and it is much different than the brand being peddled by modern "word" preachers. Consider what God says about the suffering believers who are commended for their faith in Hebrews 11: "Of whom the world was not worthy" (v. 38, NKJV). "And all these, having obtained a good testimony through faith…" (v. 39, NKJV).

No sincere preacher of God's Word will reject what God commends. No preacher has the right to preach only what he wants to preach—only what is positive and popular. A true man of God will not assume the right to be a "spiritual specialist" who majors only on positive, popular subjects. A preacher with integrity will preach what God requires him to preach, not what he wants to preach. The apostles of the New Testament did not sell themselves to prosperity and popularity. They loved the whole Word of God, and they preached the whole counsel of God.

> All Scripture is given by inspiration of God, and is profitable for doctrine, for reproof, for correction, for instruction in righteousness, that the man of God may be complete, thoroughly equipped for every good work.
> —2 TIMOTHY 3:16–17, NKJV

The faith message of the New Testament bears little resemblance to that preached by popular, prosperous word of faith preachers today. The men and women of faith in the New Testament did not make material prosperity the status symbol of faith. In fact many of them, because of their faith, lost all their material goods:

> But recall the former days in which, after you were illuminated, you endured a great struggle with sufferings, partly while you were made a spectacle both by reproaches and tribulations, and partly while you became companions of those who were so treated; for you had compassion on me in my chains, and joyfully accepted the plundering of your goods, knowing that you have a better and an enduring possession for yourselves in heaven.
> —Hebrews 10:32–34, nkjv

The scriptures we have considered are ignored by the leaders of the modern Word of Faith movement. How can they call themselves "word" preachers? The Bible presents a different gospel—one that does not deny or disdain the sufferings of faith. The truth teaches us that we overcome by faith and that we are more than conquerors who obtain victory that overcomes the world by faith; but it does not teach us that faith guarantees material prosperity and comfort in this world. The truth does not teach us that we are exempted from suffering by faith; but some of the most famous preachers in America beg to differ. What will you believe: the clear teaching of the Word of God or the distorted teaching of your favorite faith preacher?

It should not be necessary to try to convince anyone reading these thoughts that the modern faith and prosperity message is different than the message of faith preached and lived in the New Testament. A cursory reading of Acts and the Epistles will clearly reveal the differences. A man's life eventually reflects the message he preaches and follows. There is no question that the lifestyles of the apostles and preachers of the New Testament church were much different than the lavish lifestyles of the famous preachers of the modern Word of Faith movement. The well-known leaders of the New Testament church, especially the apostles, could have lived among the rich and the famous of their day had they wanted to. They chose not to. Why? They didn't sell out to the god of Mammon. They followed the example of Jesus. Jesus could have been born in a palace. He could have lived like a king. He chose to be born in a stable. He chose to live, not as a ruler, but as a servant leader. He didn't have to live that way, but He did. We should ask ourselves why and examine our attitudes and lifestyles with His in mind. Jesus could have lived more extravagantly than the most famous word of faith preacher in the world. He chose not to. He must have had a good reason for that choice. With that understanding, how should we then live? Who should we imitate? Jesus said, "Foxes have holes and birds of the air have nests, but the Son of Man has nowhere to lay His head" (Matt. 8:20, NKJV).

Was Jesus poor? No. He was rich in faith. His level of faith made all the wealth in heaven's storehouse available to Him. He was unlimited in His potential to prosper. He could have become the wealthiest minister on the planet before He even launched His ministry. Had He been willing to compromise and sell out, Satan would have helped Him to prosper. Here is the temptation Satan presented to Jesus in Matthew 4:8–9: "Again, the devil took him to a very high mountain and showed him all the kingdoms of the world and their splendor. 'All this I will give you,' he said, 'if you will bow down and worship me.'" Jesus wasn't moved by power and prosperity in this world. He did not compromise because He was not for sale. Here is His response to the devil's desperate offer: "Jesus said to him, 'Away from me, Satan! For it is written: 'Worship the Lord your God, and serve him only'" (Matt. 4:10).

Jesus didn't want the devil's kingdoms or anything that pertained to them. He didn't need them. He had faith and the promises of God. He didn't seek financial seeds from the masses that followed Him. He didn't take from them and promise a miracle harvest in return. He didn't take because He was different than many of the covetous leaders who claim to follow Him. He didn't take from His followers, and He certainly didn't use gimmicks to con them. It was against His nature; He was a giver, not a taker. Unlike many leaders of the modern faith movement, Jesus actually believed and practiced what He preached. His teaching was reinforced by His life. There were no contradictions. He didn't live like the wealthy leaders of the modern church because He didn't want to. He mingled with the poor and common people and taught that it is better to give than to receive (Acts 20:35). And His reason for giving was not just so He could reap a miracle harvest of money in return.

The poor heard Him gladly because they felt His compassion. They didn't feel like second class citizens when they were around Him. They didn't leave His presence feeling as though He cared more about their money than He did their souls. When a crowd of over five thousand people was without food, He didn't ask everyone to sow a seed for their need. His faith acted on the meager lunch of a small boy and produced enough to feed the entire crowd (John 6:4–14). When Jesus needed to pay taxes He didn't ask His followers to sow a seed to meet His need. He just told Peter to go to a certain place, catch a fish, and take money out of its mouth to pay the taxes (Matt. 17:27). Do you for one moment doubt that He could have lived more luxuriously than all the prosperity preachers of our day? If He could multiply bread and fish, He could have multiplied money—but He didn't. A man who moves with that level of faith and power never has to live modestly and identify with the lower class—unless He chooses to.

The three kings from the East who came to behold Him at Bethlehem may have given Him a small fortune. It is possible that wealthy people supported Him. Money follows miracles—even phony ones. I don't doubt that some of the wealthy people Jesus helped would have been able to sow big seeds into His ministry. But Jesus wasn't like modern faith preachers. He didn't seek seeds or sell miracles. You can turn miracles into money—if your character will allow you to do it. That is why so many unscrupulous preachers throughout history have tried to stage or manufacture them. The difference between Jesus and many modern "faith healers" (in addition to the fact that His miracles were genuine 100 percent of the time) is that He didn't use miracles to exploit people and raise offerings. He performed real miracles with one motive: love for people in need. The point to note here is that Jesus, though He had the power to be the richest person on the planet, chose not to hang out with or live the life of the rich and famous. Instead, He chose to identify with and move among the common people and the poor and oppressed. He was not like the modern leaders of the Word of Faith movement: He didn't think like them, talk like them, act like them, or live like them. Why? He didn't want to. Should we?

Chapter 3

BROTHER LOVE'S TRAVELING SALVATION SHOW

Neil Diamond made history and upset Christians nationwide with his 1969 hit "Brother Love's Travelling Salvation Show."[1] My hippie friends and I loved the song; we wore the record out. Churches and Christian organizations boycotted the song and the artist because they felt it mocked evangelicals. I still remember Diamond's response to all the criticism. He claimed that he never intended to upset Christians. He had actually been deeply moved by what he saw and felt at a tent revival. He was taken by the charisma of the evangelist and his ability to move the crowd. The song came out of that experience.

There are a lot of "traveling salvation shows" today and the biggest one is all about love. But it's not the 1960s tent revival kind of love that Neil Diamond sang about. It is love that has difficulty saying words like *sin*. It is love that lost all its convictions. Watching "Brother Love" on television makes me wonder: Have we, in the name of love, sacrificed passion and power on the altars of popularity and political correctness? Has the modern church become a bit too infatuated with entertaining speakers who peddle love? Is he a preacher or a motivational speaker? If he is a motivational speaker, let him be and calmly go on your way. But if he claims to be a preacher, pray—pray hard—for American Christianity. And as you pray ask: If he refuses to preach the whole counsel of God, if he chokes on three letter words like *sin,* is it even legal to call him a preacher?

If you got through the previous paragraph, you know that I am not trying to "win friends and influence people." I am now on ground where angels, and mice who masquerade as men of God, fear to tread. I am not ignorant. I know that to question superstars will result in my "losing friends and infuriating people." But somebody on this side of the fence has to do it. I am growing tired of letting the Bible Answer Man increase his following by questioning things we should have questioned long ago ourselves. If you regularly tune in to Brother Love's Traveling Salvation Show, I may lose you in this chapter. But trust me, if you are an enamored fan, you need to grit your teeth and forge ahead.

This chapter is designed to make you think. If you don't want to do the hard work of thinking, handle the book very carefully and run quickly back to the store to ask for a refund. If you choose to read on, I want you to do it with your eyes wide open. I am going to the deep end of the pool to jump off the high dive in this chapter. If you don't drown in the next few pages, you should have no problem swimming through the rest of the book.

Dare I touch the superstars? Oh, why not. Somebody

needs to ask a few questions. But, I wonder, will his devotees rise to scream in unison, "Touch not God's anointed"?

Does not integrity still demand that real preachers proclaim the whole counsel of God? Is there a prototype anywhere in the Bible for preachers who have forgotten how to say *sin*? The Apostle John is known as the love guy in the New Testament, but his Gospel and first Epistle are filled with references to sin. References to sin come in the same package as references to love. Is there such a thing as real love that refuses to boldly speak "the truth, the whole truth, and nothing but the truth, so help me God"? Is it true love if it refuses to speak the truth with force and conviction?

Throughout history, most of those who earned the title of false prophet were normally not the stereotypical wild-eyed nutcases who everyone calls crazy? More often they have been pleasant, smooth talking purveyors of positive messages of love, peace, and prosperity. We should have learned from Jeremiah. Such prophets were everywhere in his day. Anyone who thinks that history does not repeat itself needs to look at our modern predicament through Jeremiah's eyes. The conditions are uncannily similar. Jeremiah was grieved over the evil in the midst of God's people. He saw the coming judgment, and with a broken heart issued warning after warning; but few listened. Had Larry King interviewed Jeremiah, he would have had no difficulty saying a word that many modern day preachers choke on: *sin*.

Jeremiah cried and called people to repentance and multitudes hated him for it. But they were enamored with the positive love preachers who scratched them wherever they had an itch. Where was God in all of this? Does history reveal whose side He came down on? Let me answer that question with a question: Does anyone remember the names of the false prophets who preached peace and prosperity to a backslidden people? Do any books of the Bible bear their names? Preaching positive messages of love, when the nation is racing toward disaster, may make you popular with backslidden believers who don't want to face the reality of impending judgment; but it will eventually get you in big trouble with a holy God. History, and the God of history, has vindicated the weeping prophet who dared to confront what was popular. He dared because his love for the truth produced holy hatred for all that was false.

> "My heart within me is broken Because of the prophets.... For both prophet and priest are profane: Yes, in My house I have found their wickedness," says the LORD. "Therefore their way shall be to them Like slippery ways; in the darkness they shall be driven on And fall in them; For I will bring disaster on them.... They... caused my people... to err.... They commit adultery and walk in lies; They also strengthen the hands of evildoers, So that no one turns back from his wickedness."... Thus says the LORD of hosts: "Do not listen to the words of the prophets who prophesy to you. They make you worthless; They speak a vision of their own heart, Not from the mouth of the LORD. They continually say to those who despise Me, 'The LORD has said, "You shall have peace"... No evil shall come upon you.' I have not sent these prophets, yet they ran. I have not spoken to them, yet they prophesied. But

if they had stood in My counsel, And had caused My people to hear My words, Then they would have turned them from their evil way and from the evil of their doings.... Therefore behold, I am against the prophets," says the LORD, "who steal My words every one from his neighbor. Behold I am against the prophets," says the LORD, "who use their tongues and say, 'He says.' Behold, I am against those who prophesy false dreams,'" says the LORD, "and tell them, and cause My people to err by their lies and recklessness. Yet I did not send them or command them; therefore they shall not profit this people at all," says the LORD.
—JEREMIAH 23:9, 11–14, 16–17, 21–22, 30–32, NKJV

Polite, politically correct preachers don't like Jeremiah's approach. If he were here today, they would never think of inviting him to speak. But God's Word introduces us to real preachers who confront sin and turn people from their evil ways. How can that happen if love has lost all its convictions and power has been sacrificed on the altars of relevance? How can that happen if polite, politically correct purveyors of love do not possess the power to open their mouths and say *sin* to audiences of multiplied millions on international television? Would the Apostle Paul, or any of the authentic preachers of the New Testament, have passed on an opportunity to address the sin problem and offer a Savior before such a great audience? How can you turn people from their sins if you don't have enough conviction in your heart to so much as say the word? Please think for a moment: Can you find a prototype for such a "preacher" in the entire Bible?

I was recently asked if I liked a popular "preacher" of our day. I responded, "What's not to like? He tells me how great I am and reminds me over and over how much God loves me. He tells me I am a champion and makes me feel good about myself. I have never heard him so much as hint that I might need to repent of sin which might have offended a holy God. Why would I not like him?"

But is that the right question? Should I like a preacher who would let me go to hell without ever telling me that I was a sinner who needed to repent? The devil does that and I don't like him. The modern church is filled with people like "Brother Love." They are for everything and not against anything. They are ready for universalism which accepts all religions and refuses to condemn anything as false. It is all about the positive karma of love, love, love. But that kind of love is not what is found in the Bible. The love revealed by Jesus in the Bible is rooted in the Spirit of truth. It is against everything that is false and possesses strong convictions that will not wilt in the war against evil. Jesus was love wrapped in a human body; yet He preached with force against sin and called people to repentance. Any true preacher of the gospel follows His example.

Brother Love and his disciples are closer to the teachings of the positive gurus of Hinduism who advocate oneness with everything than they are to the Bible, which is not one with anything outside of the love and holiness embodied and revealed in Jesus. The practitioners of eastern mysticism would have no problem embracing his sweet gospel that loves everything and refuses to stand against anything. Here is what researcher and author Barbara Harris

Whitfield, a Western fan of Eastern religion, had to say in a blog of the Kundalini Research Network: "Spiritual awakenings are universal, *include everyone* and exclude no one. They include all beliefs, are *anti nothing*, *require no allegiance* and *embrace all*" (emphasis is as it appeared in the article).[2] Her "anti nothing" ideas mesh well with Brother Love's philosophy.

In spite of the unpleasant conversation that followed my response to the friend who asked me if I liked the incredibly popular "Brother Love," I am going to ask you, dear reader, what I asked her: "What's not to like?" But, again, is that really even the correct question? Should we listen to a preacher and believe his words because he has a charming smile, a pleasant personality, and an entertaining presentation; or should we be a little more concerned about the content of his message?

The false prophets with whom men of God like Elijah, Isaiah, Jeremiah, and Ezekiel contended sacrificed truth on the altars of prosperity and popularity. Compromise bought those of Elijah's day favor with the wicked Queen Jezebel. Their compromise made them very prosperous men. They were wined and dined at the queen's table for many years, but in the end their compromise cost them dearly. They had a bad day on Mount Carmel when one despised baldheaded prophet called them out. He publicly humiliated and then executed eight hundred fifty of them at the Brook Kidron (see 1 Kings 18:16–40). God does not smile on those who dilute or pervert truth in the pursuit of prosperity and popularity. Those who do so would be wise to bill themselves as motivational speakers instead of preachers; God holds preachers to a higher standard.

Brother Love often speaks to large crowds of happy ticket holders throughout the nation. Positive motivational talks have worked well for him. Sacrificing truth and avoiding the use of words like *sin* and *repentance* has made him popular with millions of devotees worldwide. But will there be a day of reckoning a little farther down the road? Will his sugar coated gospel buy him a future appointment with a modern day Elijah? Are he and his loyal lightweights any better than the prophets who fared so sumptuously at Jezebel's table? I wonder if they thought that the years of comfort and luxury were worth it when they saw the Brook Kidron run red with the blood of their comrades.

Brother Love is one of the spiritual specialists. He confines himself to carefully selected areas of truth—all positive. Are authentic preachers allowed to do that? Medical doctors do it for good reason: specialists make the big bucks. General practitioners don't normally fare as well. For some specialists, it's all about the money.

Is it acceptable for a preacher to be a love specialist, or a grace specialist, or a faith specialist, or a fire specialist, or a prophecy specialist, or a church growth specialist? Are we allowed to preach one truth to the neglect of others? Or, does the Lord insist that real preachers proclaim the whole counsel of God? "For I have not shunned to declare to you the whole counsel of God" (Acts 20:27, NKJV). That is what the preachers throughout the Bible did; and all of the real ones knew how to say *sin*. Given the opportunity to respond to a famous interviewer's questions about specific sins, they would have left his head spinning. You would have seen him stutter and cry, "Commercial break!

Commercial break!" It is a no brainer, man. Real preachers know how to say *sin* and they join prophets like Jeremiah in his attempts to turn God's people from their evil ways.

Spiritual specialists, by emphasizing one truth to the neglect of others, create an imbalance in doctrine and lifestyle. Without a broader understanding that takes in the whole counsel of God, believers will not be solidly grounded in Scripture and will be more easily deceived by seducing spirits. The Apostle Paul understood this danger and, therefore, handled the Word of God reverently and carefully. He continually emphasized the importance of sound teaching and the importance of balance in doctrine and practice. Consider his discourse to the elders from Ephesus who came to meet him at Miletus (Malta). It begins with the verse referenced in the last paragraph.

> For I have not shunned to declare unto you all the counsel of God. Take heed therefore unto yourselves, and to all the flock, over which the Holy Ghost hath made you overseers, to feed the church of God, which he hath purchased with his own blood. For I know this, that after my departing shall grievous wolves enter in among you, not sparing the flock. Also of your own selves shall men arise, speaking perverse things, to draw away disciples after them. Therefore watch, and remember, that by the space of three years I ceased not to warn every one night and day with tears.
> —Acts 20:27–31, kjv

No intelligent person would question the depth of Paul's love for Jesus or for those entrusted to his care by Jesus. He sacrificed on their behalf; he labored fervently in order to supply his own needs while ministering to them. He wept over them day and night in prayer, and he warned them of impending danger. When is the last time you heard a warning pass through the lips of Brother Love? One need not wonder how Paul would have felt about this gospel that is too polite to confront evil and warn the deceived. He would consider it perverse; and he would address its proponents as he did those who preached an aberration of the true gospel in Galatia. Paul challenged both a gospel of legalism that produced bondage and a gospel of liberalism that caused people to think they had been given a license to sin. He was not nice to those who added to or took away from the true gospel.

"But there are some…who want to pervert the gospel of Christ. But even if we, or an angel from heaven, preach any other gospel to you than what we have preached to you, let him be accursed" (Gal. 1:7–8, NKJV). And for emphasis, he repeated himself: "As we have said before, so now I say again, if anyone preaches any other gospel to you than what you have received, let him be accursed" (v. 9, NKJV).

Paul understood the danger of listening to a preacher who carelessly handles the Word of God. He realized that excessive emphasis on one area of truth, while underemphasizing others, would create imbalance that could eventually lead to full-blown heresy. Paul and Peter had their differences, but they were on the same page on the subject of deceivers: "But there were also false prophets among the people, even as there will be false teachers among you…" (2 Pet. 2:1, NKJV). Peter's Epistles are filled with warnings and admonitions to live pure and holy lives. In 2 Peter 3:17 he warned, "You therefore, beloved, since you know this beforehand, beware lest you also fall from your own steadfastness, being led away with the error of the wicked" (NKJV).

Anyone with a basic understanding of the Bible knows that God has many wonderful attributes, the chief being love and holiness. He says, "Be holy, for I am holy," in 1 Peter 1:16 (NKJV). John simply says, "...for God is love" (1 John 4:8, NKJV). It is difficult to understand how anyone with an understanding of the holiness of God could constantly preach positive motivational messages of faith and love yet seldom, if ever, confront sin and call people to repentance. Any discerning believer who has watched or listened to Brother Love should have a few questions. He presents a positive motivational message that does not address sin or the need for a savior. He preaches nothing that would bring real conviction of sin or give an understanding of why repentance is even necessary. He leads them in a prayer to receive Jesus without even explaining why they need a Savior.

Brother Love is imitated by preachers everywhere. We have a generation of preachers who are all about being positive, polite, and loving. They don't confront sin because that would not be politically correct; it would make people feel uncomfortable. Is it possible that this is the work of seducing spirits? Could it be doing more harm than good? What happens to people when preachers pronounce them "born again" before they have even heard why they need a savior? What happens when people, who have never been convicted of sin and, therefore, have never truly repented of sin, pray to receive Jesus? Is it possible that those people might not be saved at all—that instead of salvation, they have received a false hope based on the words of preachers who did not bother to clearly explain the way of salvation?

Is it too much of a stretch to think that these people will begin attending church and learn to act like Christians even though they were never properly introduced to Christ? Would it not be wise for us to consider what Brother Love and his imitators are doing in light of what great men of God like Billy Graham and David Wilkerson did for so many years? Billy Graham has probably lived with more integrity than any well-known preacher of modern times. He is without question the world's senior statesman of evangelism. Has anyone ever heard Billy Graham invite someone to receive Jesus without hearing him first clearly explain the way of salvation?

And what of Wilkerson? My heart became more burdened for the lost and hurting every time I was in his presence. He inspired me early in my ministry to witness to desperate people who others had given up on. His influence motivated me to establish a drug rehabilitation ministry patterned after Teen Challenge. Drug users and alcoholics in Teen Challenge centers throughout the world were delivered by embracing a real gospel that called them to repentance before pronouncing them born again. They repented of their sin because they were convicted of their sin. They received Jesus, not just so they could live great lives now, but so they could be forgiven through the power of the blood and be delivered from hell on earth. A candy coated gospel of low cost love would have bounced off their hardened hearts. Many of them are preachers today because of the influence of David Wilkerson on their lives. I learned from him that the real gospel deals with sin and calls people to radical discipleship. And I learned that real preachers speak the truth in love without compromise—even at the cost of criticism and rejection and the loss of popularity and prosperity. David Wilkerson knew a lot about real love, but he knew nothing of the kind of love that is married to a diluted sweet water gospel that doesn't carry enough conviction to say *sin*.

Brother Love's gospel is all sugar and no salt. It is a one-sided gospel that lacks scriptural substance and supernatural power. It has no holy influence on secular society or pagan culture. Are we deluded? Why would anyone with a remote understanding of the authentic gospel preached in the New Testament be so impressed with entertaining motivational messages? Have we become so enamored with the rich and the famous, so impressed with success and numbers, that we have been drained of all discernment?

Paul said that the gospel of the deceivers is "no gospel at all" (Gal. 1:7). There is no substance to it. It doesn't have the power to save a flea. Is Brother Love's diluted gospel any different? When did we begin believing that saying a little prayer at the end of a motivational talk could get someone saved? His gospel is more palatable than what the legalistic Judaizers[3] of Paul's day preached—but are the results any different? Every serious student of Scripture knows that the legalism of the Judaizers won't bring anybody to Jesus. Is the same not true of liberalism that emphasizes love to the neglect of holiness? The gospel preached by Brother Love and his loyal lightweights is all sugar and no salt. Too much of a good thing can become a bad thing. Too much refined white sugar will bless you with diabetes and kill you before your time. A sugar coated gospel will have the same effect spiritually. It won't produce the bitter bondage of the legalists; you will die with a sweet taste in your mouth, but the result will be the same—bitter taste or sweet—you will still be spiritually dead.

Candy coated Christianity is for lightweights who are more concerned about feeling good than they are about fulfilling the Great Commission. The Apostle Paul would have spit on this candy coated religion. This is not the gospel of the New Testament. It produces a self-centered, watered-down Christianity that caters to those who love the things of this world. It doesn't sound like the gospel Jesus preached. It won't challenge converts to become devoted disciples who lay their lives down for the gospel's sake nor take up their cross daily to follow Jesus. Converts who listen to this sweet water gospel don't even consider making such commitments; their favorite "preacher" has never bothered to tell them that Jesus demands it. They are following a sweet talking icon who seldom, if ever, uses words like sacrifice, commitment, sin, repentance, or hell. Without mentioning the biblical requirements of discipleship, he invites multitudes to come to Jesus. This is not the same gospel the disciples preached.

How would that have worked for Peter, or John, or Paul? Perhaps we should at least look at the teachings of Brother Love against the backdrop of how these great men of faith lived and preached: "...and when they had called for the apostles and beaten them, they commanded that they should not speak in the name of Jesus, and let them go. So they departed from the presence of the council, rejoicing that they were counted worthy to suffer shame for His name" (Acts 5:40–41, NKJV).

What if I told you that each those apostles lived his best life now? They weren't living them without a cross or conviction on the sweet syrup of positive Christianity; they were living them on the high protein of the great honor of being counted worthy to suffer for the name of Jesus. In their minds, the good life was not one of worldly success and comfort but of complete surrender to Jesus and total abandonment to the will of God. It was not only the apostles who lived that way. The deacons demanded the right to lay down their lives too. Stephen didn't dilute his message when a mob became angry; and he didn't recant when they took him out of town to stone him:

> When they heard these things they were cut to the heart, and they gnashed at him with their teeth. But he being full of the Holy Spirit, gazed into heaven and saw the glory of God, and Jesus standing at the right hand of God, and said, "Look! I see heaven opened and the Son of Man standing at the right hand of God!" Then they cried with a loud voice, stopped their ears, and ran at him with one accord: and they cast him out of the city and stoned him.
> —Acts 7:54–58, nkjv

You won't find pleasant preachers with a seducing gospel of the good life in the New Testament. The authors of the Gospels were real men of God who were ready to give their blood at any moment for the glory of the Lamb. What modern preachers call sacrifice, they called privilege. The men who gave us the Bible were not soft, selfish lovers of pleasure. Their hearts beat with love for Jesus, and that love knew how to be violent with anything that dishonored

Him. They were much more interested in glory than gain; and in pursuit of the glory of God they were willing to embrace pain, sacrifice, and suffering without complaint.

I don't have the boldness of Paul; but I have enough disdain for this pathetic, sugar coated aberration of the gospel to at least publicly question it. Paul would have done more; he would have spit on it. He would have condemned it, and he would have challenged its supporters to repent and return to the truth. Listen to him in Philippians 3:7–8 and 10 and ask yourself if he was not different than the lightweights of our day:

> But what things were gain to me, these I have counted loss for Christ.... I also count all things loss for the excellence of the knowledge of Christ Jesus my Lord, for whom I have suffered the loss of all things, and count them as rubbish [*dung* in KJV], that I may gain Christ.... that I may know Him and the power of His resurrection, and the fellowship of His sufferings, being conformed to His death.
> —PHILIPPIANS 3:7–8, 10, NKJV

Paul wasn't endeavoring to live the good life now. In fact, he wasn't endeavoring to live at all; he was endeavoring to daily die that Christ might live His life through him. Paul's life and teaching are an affront to this pleasant sounding gospel. Listen to his words in the following scriptures. Let them erase all doubt as to whether there is any substance in this deceptively sweet, unholy perversion of the true gospel of Christ:

> I beseech you therefore brethren, by the mercies of God, that you present your bodies a living sacrifice,

holy, acceptable to God, which is your reasonable service.
—ROMANS 12:1, NKJV

I have been crucified with Christ; It is no longer I who live, but Christ lives in me; and the life which I now live in the flesh I live by faith in the Son of God, who loved me and gave Himself for me....But God forbid that I should boast except in the cross of our Lord Jesus Christ, by whom the world has been crucified to me, and I to the world.
—GALATIANS 2:20; 6:14

Whenever I hear Brother Love or one of his loyal lightweights, I wonder how they can even consider themselves preachers. The sermons of the great preachers of the Bible and church history are so different than those of modern motivational speakers who call themselves preachers. They preached all the counsel of God and had great reverence for the Bible. They did more than encourage, inspire, and motivate with positive messages filled with sweetness. They followed the admonition of the Apostle Paul and used the Word of God to establish doctrine, reprove, correct, and instruct believers in righteousness (2 Tim. 3:16, NKJV). They used the Word of God to confront sin and call people to repentance.

Paul's sermons were nothing like the sweet motivational talks that have made modern preachers popular with enamored fans throughout the world. Paul's preaching didn't always make people feel good about themselves. Sometimes they got convicted and felt bad until they repented. Paul didn't try to create a fan club out of followers with itching ears. He didn't preach to scratch people wherever they itched. Paul was different than Brother Love. He preached what people needed to hear, not what they wanted to hear. Paul and his disciples did something very few modern preachers ever do these days: They combined warning, rebuke, and correction with encouragement and instruction. Paul instructed Timothy to: "correct, rebuke and encourage—with great patience and careful instruction" (2 Tim. 4:2). He told Titus: "rebuke them sharply, so that they will be sound in the faith" (Titus 1:13). Can you even imagine our smiling motivational speakers ever doing what Paul and the other apostles said real preachers should do?

Earlier I asked, "What's not to like?" Allow me to expand that answer. Let's see, what's not to like? How about spiritual diabetes? How about syrupy sludge sliding through your spiritual arteries? How about serious spiritual sickness from an imbalanced diet laced with sweets and junk food? How about spiritual declension and debilitation that leaves you so weak you are afraid to say "Boo!" to the puniest little demon in the pack? If we don't give up our love for sweets, if we don't stop drinking at the sweet water wells of compromised preachers, we won't be in shape for the fight that is before us.

If you feed on sweet little "sermonettes" for too long, you will become a sweet little "Christianette." You will fall down in a fight. The devil is going to walk on sugar loving Christians. You may be playing, but he is not. I assure you once again: halfhearted Christians will be devoured by a wholehearted devil. You need a message with some meat in it now and then. This little gospel is all sugar and no salt. It doesn't have the power to convict sinners or influence them to turn from unrighteousness. If you are familiar with the teachings of Christ, you don't need me to tell you that a saltless Christian is about to have a bad day. Consider His words in Matthew 5:13: "You are the salt of the earth; but if the salt loses its flavor, how shall it be seasoned? It is then good for nothing but to be thrown out and trampled underfoot by men" (NKJV).

Christians are compared to salt. Salt is seasoning that adds spice to life. It is also a preservative. A salty Christian has a preserving influence on what is good in the culture. Almost anyone who is aware of the increasing moral decline in our nation realizes that something is corrupting the culture. Those who are more aware realize that the degree of corruption correlates with the declining influence of the church. The declining influence of the church correlates with the compromise of preachers. Where does that leave us? Is the salt losing its savor?

According to Jesus, unless the trend is reversed we will soon be good for nothing. That frightens me. You can hang out with the self-indulgent consumers of a sweet sounding gospel and drink more sugar water if you want to. I am not going to hang out with people like Brother Love because they don't really love me. If they loved me, they would tell me the truth. They wouldn't pat me on the back and tell me how great I am as I travel down the road that leads to hell. They would love me enough to say something that would wake me up, convict me of my sin, and cause me to repent.

The devil will preach positive messages and tell you that you are a champion every day. He will pat you on the back and tell you what a great person you are all the way to hell. But I am never tempted to believe that the devil loves me. People who love me tell me the truth. I am going to search for some people who have no desire for a gospel that is all sugar and no salt. I am going to find some people who realize that revival is our only hope: people who are willing to swear off sugar and fast and pray until it comes. I am going to part ways with Brother Love and his "traveling salvation show" and look for some believers who have the spirit of Elijah and the backbone of Jeremiah. I am going to search until I find some people who still believe 2 Chronicles 7:14:

> If My people who are called by My name will humble themselves, and pray and seek My face, and turn from their wicked ways, then I will hear from heaven, and will forgive their sin and heal their land.
> —2 Chronicles 7:14, nkjv

Pass the salt, please.

Chapter 4

THE SEEKER-SENSITIVE DELUSION

THE GOSPEL PREACHED by Jesus and the apostles of the early church is relevant in every generation. But many modern preachers don't think it is. They must not think the Holy Spirit is relevant either. They have restricted His movement and rejected the operation of His gifts in their services. The philosophy of the modern seeker-sensitive movement (often called seeker-friendly) is diametrically different than that of the New Testament church. Seeker-friendly proponents design church services that appeal to unchurched seekers. Services are not built around the Bible but around the likes and dislikes of a target group. Seeker-sensitive leaders work hard to create an upbeat, nonthreatening atmosphere in which the unchurched feel comfortable. Surveys are conducted to discover what people want, and then services are designed to appeal to them. Businesses do the same thing to market their products. Good salesmen try to discover what people want and then convince them to buy it. Seeker-sensitive leaders are doing the same thing; they are marketing Christianity by finding out what people want and giving it to them.

There is a major flaw in the seeker-sensitive philosophy. God doesn't adjust or alter the gospel based on what people want. He always begins with what they need. The seeker-sensitive philosophy is seriously flawed because it begins with what unchurched seekers say they want. That is a bad approach. What people want is often not what they need. The foundational ideas of seeker-sensitive philosophy are contradicted by the truth of the Bible and by the manner in which God interacts with human beings. He begins with what we need, not what we want. He doesn't allow our thinking or preferences to influence the way He relates to us. Can you imagine how the Bible would read if God had conducted surveys to determine what humans wanted Him to put in it? People want sin and the pleasures of the world, but that is not what they need. The Holy Spirit inspired and directed the writing of the Bible on the foundation of eternally existent truth. It addresses the needs of mankind and presents a holy God who is different than sinful man as the solution to those needs.

Those who recognize that God is the answer conform to His demands. When a person accepts Jesus as Savior and begins to obey His teachings, God suddenly becomes relevant. The relationship doesn't begin by God coming our way and conforming to our wants. He doesn't change or make adjustments to accommodate us. He steps into the middle of our world and presents Himself as the solution to our problems, the answer to our needs. He reveals Himself and preaches a gospel that helps us to become like Him. He has no intention of becoming like us. He doesn't change; He demands that we do. He doesn't seek relevance by conforming to our preferences and behaviors. The gospel doesn't seek conformity with anything; it demands change. Jesus did what seeker-sensitive leaders won't do: He makes demands and requires us to become real disciples. He doesn't entertain us by giving us what we want in beautiful climate controlled buildings. He begins by commanding us to repent and believe the gospel (Mark 1:15). He follows repentance and faith with an unconditional call to discipleship. He doesn't present a diluted, non-threatening gospel that entertains seekers with donuts and refreshments in the foyer until they become comfortable enough to enter the auditorium. Jesus is relevant and He really loves people, but He doesn't cater to or try to entertain anybody. He beckons us with love; but to enter into a relationship and experience that love, we must respond to His call to radical discipleship.

Jesus doesn't hang around trying to entertain us until we are comfortable enough to take a few feeble steps in His direction. He makes it plain up front: If you want to be My disciple you must deny yourself, take up your cross daily and follow Me (Mark 8:34). He demands a decision, a choice that changes everything about the way we think, act, and live. And He clearly lays out the consequences of not choosing to follow Him in true discipleship:

> For whoever wants to save their life will lose it, but whoever loses their life for me and for the gospel will save it. What good is it for someone to gain the whole world, yet forfeit their soul? Or what can anyone give in exchange for their soul?
> —Mark 8:35–37

You will never hear preaching like that in a seeker-sensitive sanctuary. It is too threatening. It is too demanding. It is too confrontational. It will make the unchurched uncomfortable. It is not relevant. Does it strike anyone as being a bit audacious for men to concoct a philosophy of ministry that begins with the premise that the gospel Jesus preached and the manner in which He presented it are not relevant? Can you see the dangers associated with embracing such a weak, diluted little gospel? Have you considered where it will lead you? I have: It will lead you to a courtroom where you will have the opportunity to present enough evidence to get you convicted for being a Christian. It may leave you standing before a Judge, who will want to know what part of "repent," and what part of "deny yourself," and what part of "take up your cross" you don't understand. The perverted seeker-sensitive philosophy may leave you standing ashamed, like the emperor who had no clothes, before the just Judge of the universe. It might result in your listening to words you never wanted to hear: "If anyone is ashamed of me and my words in this adulterous and sinful generation, the Son of Man will be ashamed of them when he comes in his Father's glory with the holy angels" (Mark 8:38). We really should examine the dangers of embracing a philosophy of ministry that has so maligned and weakened the gospel.

Jesus began His preaching ministry with a word that seeker-sensitive leaders seldom or never say: *repent*. He issued the call to discipleship with demands they will never make. They won't make them because they don't believe in the power of the relevant and authentic gospel Jesus preached. There is no other explanation for the damage they have done to it. They never would have weakened and diluted it had they possessed the power to press its claims with conviction. In seeking relevance through conformity, they have become irrelevant and powerless to impact culture. You don't change a godless culture by conforming to it. Ideas like that epitomize foolishness. And even if they become relevant, it wouldn't do any good. What good is relevance without power?

Seeker-sensitive leaders deliberately restrict the moving of the Holy Spirit. They are among those who have a form of godliness but deny its power (2 Tim. 3:5). It is foolish to think that you can have true relevance without the power of the Holy Spirit. What seeker sensitive-leaders have done to the gospel is shameful. They never would have distorted it had they believed in its power. They committed a grievous sin, a tragic error that has the potential to lead multiplied millions into eternity with a false hope.

Only arrogant or deceived leaders would require the Holy Spirit to conform to their philosophy while they conform to the wants of the world. Only arrogant or deceived leaders would take it upon themselves to dilute, distort, and dress up the gospel to make it more appealing to a world that wants to run from the demands of discipleship. They never would have done what they did to the gospel had they believed in its relevance and power. They never would have subjugated the demands of the gospel to the wants of the world if they had experienced its power in their own lives—unless they simply no longer wanted to accept or proclaim those demands. They never would have maligned it had they truly loved it—had they not been ashamed of it. It is foolish for a puny human to assume the authority to add to or take away from the glorious gospel of Christ. You can follow preachers foolish enough to dilute the gospel and restrict the Spirit, or you can line up behind leaders who talk like this: "For I am not ashamed of the gospel of Christ, for it is the power of God to salvation for everyone who believes" (Paul the Apostle in Romans 1:16, NKJV). What you choose will determine your eternal destiny.

Seeker-sensitive philosophy is nonconfrontational evangelism at its best. The Bible knows nothing of it. Believers in the New Testament church had a different philosophy and approach. They went out from the church to confront unbelievers in a hostile culture. They didn't try to bring the world to church. The methods employed by the church in the Book of Acts are the exact opposite of those practiced by the seeker-sensitive movement. The believers in the Book of Acts took the church to the world. The proponents of the seeker friendly style of evangelism bring the world to the church. New Testament believers practiced confrontational power evangelism that produced conviction and pressed for a response. Seeker-friendly advocates practice a casual, dialed-down approach that is nonconfrontational and without conviction. The difference in their low-key, no pressure approach and that practiced in the Book of Acts is obvious to any student of Scripture who is willing to take the time to compare.

The preaching of Peter on the Day of Pentecost brought conviction, called for a response, and resulted in repentance. The preaching of Stephen—or any of the preachers in the New Testament church—was not casual, seeker-friendly evangelism. It confronted people and their culture with a gospel of power that called for repentance and commitment to a new way of life. If we are looking for a model to follow, we would be wise to find it in the Bible. God set the pattern in the Gospels and the Book of Acts. I have never read anywhere that He has another plan, or that man could improve on the methods He instituted in the first church. The results speak for themselves. The greatest period of church growth in history came immediately after the Day of Pentecost. Let's contrast the preaching of Peter, Stephen, and Paul with the casual nonconfrontational style of preaching so prevalent in the modern church. There was no lack of love in the confrontational style of evangelism practiced by the early church; but in this politically correct age that approach would be considered offensive. It is not loving to confront people and cause them to feel uncomfortable. The truth is, the lack is found among people who don't love sinners enough to tell them the truth. The gospel has been so watered down that we have nearly lost the ability to confidently speak the truth in love and press for a decision.

We should compare the different results of the two styles and then be honest in answering the questions: What does the evidence imply? Which is the most effective? If we think the growth produced by the power evangelism of the early church is worth considering, and if we think the commitment of the early believers was stronger than what we see in the modern church, perhaps it is time to ask which pattern we should be following: that of Jesus and the disciples, or that of the "gurus" of the seeker-sensitive movement?

Shouldn't we factor miracles into the equation? Does

anyone doubt that the preaching and ministry of the leaders of the early church was carried out under a greater anointing and demonstrated with greater power than what we see in the church today? Why would we want to trade the excitement and power of the New Testament church for a calm, watered-down gospel that seldom sees miracles, deep conviction of sin, dramatic repentance, or conversion? How long must we endure calm, dialed-down Christianity with its lack of anointing and power before we wake up to the delusion? Why is it so difficult for modern believers to discern the difference between human ability and supernatural enablement?

How long will it take for us to understand that our churches are being filled with warm bodies, not converted sinners? How could they be converted? Many have never even been convinced that they are sinners who need the Savior. Seeker-friendly philosophy won't even allow you to call them sinners; they must be referred to as unchurched seekers, not lost sinners. How can the multitudes of seekers filling our buildings be saved if they have never been convicted of sin? And how will they repent with intelligence if they have never been convicted? And how will they exercise faith for salvation if they have never repented? How deep is this delusion?

Here is Peter on the Day of Pentecost. It will not require much discernment to recognize the difference between his message and method from that of the leaders of the modern seeker-sensitive movement.

> "Fellow Israelites, listen to this: Jesus of Nazareth was a man accredited by God to you by miracles,

wonders and signs, which God did among you through him, as you yourselves know. This man was handed over to you by God's deliberate plan and foreknowledge; and you, with the help of wicked men, put him to death by nailing him to the cross. But God raised him from the dead, freeing him from the agony of death, because it was impossible for death to keep its hold on him.... Therefore let all Israel be assured of this: God has made this Jesus, whom you crucified, both Lord and Messiah." When the people heard this, they were cut to the heart and said to Peter and the other apostles, "Brothers, what shall we do?" Peter replied, "Repent and be baptized, every one of you, in the name of Jesus Christ for the forgiveness of your sins. And you will receive the gift of the Holy Spirit. The promise is for you and your children and for all who are far off—for all whom the Lord our God will call." With many other words he warned them; and he pleaded with them, "Save yourselves from this corrupt generation." Those who accepted his message were baptized, and about three thousand were added to their number that day.

—ACTS 2:22–24, 36–41

How could we ever improve on that? What seeker-friendly preacher has seen three thousand actually converted following one of his casual, entertaining messages? What are we thinking? Are we thinking at all? Why are we so reticent to return to the pattern Jesus provided and the apostles practiced?

Stephen was a deacon in the early church. He was so diligent in his service and in his pursuit of God that he became a powerful evangelist. He had the honor of being the first martyr of the church. Stephen did not practice politically correct preaching or friendship evangelism. He would have spurned the seeker-friendly philosophy. Yet, his sermon in Acts 7:1–60 is considered by many Bible scholars to be the best sermon ever proclaimed by anyone other than Jesus. It is a concise history of God's dealings with humanity from Abraham to the early church. It didn't win him any friends, but it did influence people. It is still influencing people today. Professors of history and homiletics alike hold it up as an example and require students to study it for both content and style. Careful study of this kind of New Testament preaching would deliver us from our modern delusions and put us on the path to being "transformed by the renewing of our mind[s]" (Rom. 12:2). After considering his bold, confrontational approach in the following verses, we will undoubtedly be left wondering if this great evangelist would be welcome in the pulpits of most of the churches we attend today. Here is an excerpt from Stephen's sermon:

> You stiff-necked people! Your hearts and ears are still uncircumcised. You are just like your ancestors: You always resist the Holy Spirit! Was there ever a prophet your ancestors did not persecute? They even killed those who predicted the coming of the Righteous One. And now you have betrayed and murdered him—you who have received the law that was given through angels but have not obeyed it. When the members of the Sanhedrin heard this, they were furious and gnashed their teeth at him. But Stephen, full of the Holy Spirit, looked up to heaven and saw the glory of God, and Jesus

standing at the right hand of God. "Look," he said, "I see heaven open and the Son of Man standing at the right hand of God." At this they covered their ears and, yelling at the top of their voices, they all rushed at him, dragged him out of the city and began to stone him. Meanwhile, the witnesses laid their coats at the feet of a young man named Saul. While they were stoning him, Stephen prayed, "Lord Jesus, receive my spirit." Then he fell on his knees and cried out, "Lord, do not hold this sin against them." When he had said this, he fell asleep.

—Acts 7:51–60

Don't fail to note that what is often considered the greatest sermon preached by anyone other than Jesus was not a polite, seeker friendly motivational talk; it was the opposite. It was a convicting, "in-your-face" message that made its hearers very uncomfortable. The persecution of the church intensified after the stoning of Stephen. The believers were forced to leave Jerusalem and were scattered everywhere. But even under severe persecution, they didn't back up for the devil. They didn't go hide in the security of a seeker-friendly sanctuary and lick their wounds. They didn't lose their salt or alter their approach. They didn't exchange their confrontational, power evangelism for a more politically correct, warm and fuzzy, seeker-friendly version. If anything, they stepped up the pace and charged the gates of hell with greater force and fury. Revival broke out wherever those believers landed. They were beaten, imprisoned, fed to lions and hung on crosses like their Master. Nero dipped them in tar, hung them in his gardens and set them on fire to light up the night. During his parties, he moved among them with his honored guests and cried, "Look, the Christians are the light of the world."

Persecution didn't stop the believers of the early church. It didn't cause them to run and hide from the cruel culture that was so unkind to them. First century Christians were a little different than we in America today. They had more interest in fulfilling the Great Commission than in finding comfort in this world. Here's what Luke says about the persecuted believers after Stephen's martyrdom:

> On that day a great persecution broke out against the church in Jerusalem, and all except the apostles were scattered throughout Judea and Samaria. Godly men buried Stephen and mourned deeply for him. But Saul began to destroy the church. Going from house to house, he dragged off both men and women and put them in prison. Those who had been scattered preached the word wherever they went. Philip went down to a city in Samaria and proclaimed the Messiah there. When the crowds heard Philip and saw the signs he performed, they all paid close attention to what he said. For with shrieks, impure spirits came out of many, and many who were paralyzed or lame were healed. So there was great joy in that city.
> —Acts 8:1–7

Would any real Christian in his right mind choose the modern seeker-friendly delusion over the authentic Christianity of the Book of Acts? Those early believers did not compromise with the world and, therefore, they did not sacrifice their ability to influence the world. They were more interested in being full of the Holy Ghost and power than in being cool, culture-current, and seeker-friendly.

What was the difference between that church and the church today? They confronted and changed their culture: We avoid confrontation and, consequently, our culture is changing us. They became less worldly; we become more worldly—and we do it all in the name of seeker-friendly evangelism which advocates creating a nonthreatening atmosphere where the unchurched can feel comfortable. This is a very strong delusion.

Where did we ever get the idea that Jesus or the disciples of the New Testament would approve of a philosophy of evangelism designed to make sinners feel comfortable. They employed a much different approach. They were motivated by a stronger love. Jesus and the early disciples loved sinners enough to tell them the truth—truth that often made them uncomfortable: uncomfortable enough that their conviction led to godly sorrow, repentance and genuine faith. Leaders of the seeker-sensitive movement have propagated a delusion that says we can ignore the example set by Jesus and improve on the methods employed by the early church. They have exalted relevance over truth and the power of the Spirit. Is it truly relevance or is it just the false peace of compromise? And even if the relevance is real, what good is relevance without power?

How many of our churches are filled with people who think they are saved but have actually never been converted? They have been deceived by the same philosophy of ministry practiced by Brother Love—a philosophy that leads people in a prayer to receive Jesus without even being told why they need a savior. They have not been convicted of sin; they have not repented. But after an entertaining motivational talk, they repeat a little prayer and believe the charming preacher who tells them they are born again. They don't even know what it means to be born again, but they believe the famous preacher and begin attending church. They observe what others do, begin imitating them, and soon feel comfortable among them.

This is one of the greatest dangers of the seeker-friendly delusion. It is filling our churches with people who have never been converted yet think they are Christians. How could they be converted? They were never convicted of sin or convinced of their need for a savior. They never repented of sin because the "preacher" never told them they needed to. Consequently, there is little or no change in their lives. No wonder this delusion is so popular; you don't have to change the way you live. You just add Jesus to your life and go on your way. You can have all this and heaven too. There is no call to discipleship, no mention of taking up your cross and following Jesus, and no challenge to commitment that would cause you to lay your life down for the gospel's sake. This is not just "Christianity lite." It is a seductive delusion—a doctrine of demons that produces a false hope.

I attended the seminars of the leading seeker-friendly pastors before they were famous. I embraced the philosophy and employed its methods for about three years. When my wife Cindy and I returned from several years of missionary work in Latin America, we established another church in the St. Louis area. Within two years of preaching word of faith messages and employing seeker-friendly philosophies, I had a new building on fifteen acres of interstate property with three hundred attending on Sunday morning. It was all working just like the "gurus" said it would. I was doing great—until I was severely convicted by the Holy Spirit. I saw the delusion and humbly repented to the congregation for misleading them. That was when I realized I had a crowd but not a church.

I lost sixty people in one service. Why did they leave? They wanted a positive upbeat service. They didn't want a pastor on his knees, humbling himself before God, and repenting for preaching what people wanted to hear. In the following weeks I lost more people. My twenty-five minute "sermonettes" became forty and fifty minute messages that were too long for the unchurched seekers I had gathered. I returned to my roots and started preaching messages that were designed to produce conviction—not condemnation, but conviction. I challenged people to repent, return to their first love, and enter into deeper commitment. Many didn't want to be challenged or convicted. They wanted me to scratch them wherever they itched.

I started reminding people that Jesus called us to live righteously and be a light to those in darkness. I preached that Jesus gave us the Great Commission, not the "Great Suggestion." Some got upset because they felt that I was pressuring them. I reminded them that Jesus said some challenging things about discipleship, and that He pressed for a response to His preaching. They didn't want to hear that He required His followers to deny themselves, take up their crosses, and follow Him daily (Mark 8:34). That was negative, "over the top" preaching and they didn't want to be bothered with it. I could go on and on, but it would probably help you more to simply understand why

I became convicted and left the comfortable, warm and fuzzy world of seeker- friendly Christianity.

I changed course when I realized that I was under a delusion. It became clear to me that in the pursuit of success I had departed from the simplicity of the authentic gospel. I was compelled to honestly face the truth that I had deliberately diluted the message to make it more appealing. I was preaching a gospel designed to entertain and make people feel comfortable. I realized that I had exchanged the love that had once produced a sincere burden for lost souls for a love that had lost a lot of its convictions. Being cool and culture-current had become more important than preaching "Jesus Christ and him crucified" in the power of the Spirit (1 Cor. 2:2).

The lights went on for me at a seminar outside Chicago. I had listened to talks about marketing the church and what "unchurched Harry" and "unchurched Mary" liked and didn't like. I had listened to teachings on the importance of never telling people what they ought to do, and especially never preaching about what they ought not to do. I had heard about the importance of everyone on the platform being color coordinated. I had heard enough! Ministry had become mechanical. Preaching had become a refined science designed to be pleasant and entertaining. It all appealed to my brain, but my spirit was troubled. Suddenly I was haunted by a rather important recurring question: Is this scriptural?

The deal was sealed for me when the pastor of the seeker-friendly megachurch made this statement: "If you want your church to grow, you have to face the reality that you cannot allow verbal manifestations of the Holy Spirit in your worship services?" I felt nauseous. I was scared. I wondered if lightning might strike at any moment. Here was a puny human being telling other puny human beings that we could tell the omniscient, omnipresent, omnipotent Spirit of God when and how He could move. How did we get here? What kind of delusion could bring sincere preachers to such a place? I made the decision at that moment that it was over for me: no more seminars and ideas rooted in human wisdom and excellence; no more trying to imitate methods that had produced what seemed to be success for another man. I made up my mind that I was returning to the clear teaching of the Bible and that I would no longer embrace anything that did not have clear scriptural precedent.

The teaching at the seminar that afternoon was followed by a question and answer period. There were several hundred leaders in attendance from a wide range of backgrounds, including a good number of Pentecostal and charismatic pastors who were my seniors. I was certain that one of them would ask for clarification on the statement about no church growth if the gifts of the spirit were allowed to operate. But all of the questions were practical and had to do with the mechanics of church growth and management. It dawned on me that we were running out of time and no one was going to raise the question that was haunting me. I knew it would be controversial but I also knew I was convicted and I could not remain silent. I stood and asked for clarification on the statement before I presented my question. He affirmed that he did indeed believe that you would not experience church growth if you allowed verbal manifestations of the Spirit in your worship services. The surveys they had conducted at that time indicated that it would turn off unchurched seekers. I then asked, "Would you please respond to that statement with the Book of Acts as a backdrop?" He didn't like my question. The conference room became very quiet. It was a touché moment, and I was on his turf. I didn't care. I didn't want to grieve the precious Holy Spirit a moment longer.

His answer was not an answer and it really is not worth repeating, but I won't leave you hanging. Here it is: "Different strokes for different folks." I didn't back off; I told him I would like an honest attempt at an answer. He never did give a real answer to my question—he didn't have one. Part of his non-answer was that the baptism in the Holy Spirit was not for everybody. I disagreed; a guy named Peter who I have a lot of respect for said it was for everybody: "The promise is for you and your children and for all who are far off—for all whom the Lord our God will call" (Acts 2:39).

I left with resolve to return to New Testament Christianity and yield as fully as possible to the control of the Holy Spirit. Since that conference, I have endeavored to follow His direction and preach the whole counsel of God. I no longer dilute the gospel to make it more appealing. I endeavor to speak to please God and not men. Most of my friends who were at that conference with me continued their journey on the seeker-sensitive train and some have experienced numerical growth. But I wonder if we really want to reduce Christianity to a numbers game? Has everyone forgotten the inflated claims and the inaccurate statistics of the much hyped church growth movement? What will be the lasting fruit of the seeker-sensitive philosophy?

You may have a crowd, you may have success in the eyes of man; but, if you have pushed the Holy Spirit to the perimeters, what do you really have? Does the Holy Spirit even attend the services? Does He go where He is not wanted? Is much of what we call success today just on the surface? Is this popular dialed-down philosophy producing real disciples or is it producing Christians who are an inch deep and a mile wide? Is it producing true disciples or just numbers that allow us to put more notches on our gospel guns? Is it true success, or have we come under a strong delusion? Can there be true success in a church where the Holy Spirit is not in control and sometimes not even allowed to move? What good is relevance without power?

Let's briefly review some of the key beliefs and practices of the seeker-friendly or seeker-sensitive philosophy of evangelism and church growth and then look at a few more passages from the Book of Acts. A common practice among seeker-friendly churches is to conduct neighborhood surveys. Those surveys are designed to discover what the unchurched like and don't like about church. Data from surveys often indicate that people prefer shorter, more positive sermons, less talk about money, upbeat music, and a casual comfortable atmosphere. They want to come to a church service that doesn't feel like a church service. They prefer a pleasant, mild-mannered preacher who doesn't raise his voice much or get too excited. Seeker-friendly pastors are expected to be polite, politically correct, cool, and relevant.

Things the unchurched don't like are naturally the opposite of these, but we will state some of them for greater clarity. They don't like long or loud messages that emphasize repentance or demand change. They don't like to be convicted or told what they should or shouldn't do. Most who respond to the surveys, with the exception of the elderly, usually mention that they don't like outdated songs. Anything considered to be negative is a problem. Sadly, this can include references to the blood of Jesus, the cross, sacrifice, or suffering for the gospel's sake. Theological terms such as redemption and justification are considered outdated. Preachers don't try to honestly teach and explain them; they just find ways to express such theological terms in more relevant, culture-current terminology.

We could go on and on, but I think the point has been made. Things change over time. Cultures change and the cultural norms of one generation are rejected and replaced by later generations. But I think Christians must be very careful here. The kingdom of God is our culture. It transcends all other cultures. The revolutionary message of the New Testament is still relevant today. The gospel has not changed. The message is the same as it was when Jesus introduced it. But what about the approach? It is also relevant today. It would be difficult—actually impossible—to improve on the simple methods of evangelism and discipleship practiced by Jesus and His followers. In fact, churches in modern nations that are experiencing the greatest revivals and growth are still practicing them.

Seeker-friendly evangelism was not practiced in China during the great revival there; but the growth, strength, and depth of commitment of the church in China greatly surpasses ours. Under communist persecution pastors were not able to create comfortable, nonthreatening environments for the unchurched. The great revival in China resulted from the application of simple New Testament principles and methods of evangelism and discipleship.

The truth is: the principles and methods taught by Jesus are relevant in any culture, at any time in history. The gospel of the New Testament, and the philosophies and methods with which it advanced, are as effective today as they were two thousand years ago. They are still culture current. They still produce real disciples. Jesus was never interested in simply filling up buildings and entertaining Christians in a comfortable environment. He came to start a revolution that would result in the overthrow and destruction of the kingdom of darkness. Jesus was not a pleasant, mild-mannered, seeker-sensitive preacher. He and His followers preached the gospel with boldness and great power, and in the process they made a lot of people angry and uncomfortable. Jesus didn't give us a commission to go into all the world to erect beautiful climate controlled buildings and create comfortable atmospheres that appeal to the unchurched. He sent us out with authority to attack hell and release its prisoners. He sent us out to preach a gospel of power with force and conviction.

There is not a prototype of a pleasant seeker-sensitive preacher anywhere in the Bible—unless you look among the false prophets. The followers of Jesus were sold out soldiers who were willing to sacrifice and suffer gladly for the gospel. They didn't retreat into the security of comfortable sanctuaries. They advanced as the army of God in the earth and cared little for entertaining services on the playgrounds of religion. They fiercely attacked the kingdom of darkness and confronted its prisoners with a gospel that had the power to deliver them. The modern seeker-friendly gospel would not survive for a minute on the front lines of this battlefield. It would be helpless in a wrestling match with the principalities and powers of darkness. The seeker-friendly gospel is a fragile thing that only works in prosperous nations that can provide it with beautiful, climate controlled buildings where it can entertain the interested. It doesn't even seek the baptism of power required by the followers of Jesus in the early church. How have we become so deluded that we are actually impressed by success produced through human excellence without the help of the Holy Spirit?

Jesus didn't tell us to wait in Jerusalem until we had the funds to erect huge buildings where the unchurched could be entertained by teachers willing to scratch them wherever they itched. He came to build an army of radical believers who would be ready without hesitation to sacrifice everything for the gospel's sake. He didn't come to gather huge crowds of halfhearted seekers. He came to build an army of sold-out soldiers who would attack hell and prevail against it. The following verses reveal how the early church operated. Have we departed from the pattern?

> After his suffering, he presented himself to them and gave many convincing proofs that he was alive. He appeared to them over a period of forty days and spoke about the kingdom of God. On one occasion, while he was eating with them, he gave them this command: "Do not leave Jerusalem, but wait for

the gift my Father promised, which you have heard me speak about. For John baptized with water, but in a few days you will be baptized with the Holy Spirit.... But you will receive power when the Holy Spirit comes on you; and you will be my witnesses in Jerusalem, and in all Judea and Samaria, and to the ends of the earth."
—Acts 1:3–5, 8

Demonstrations of power were common among the believers in the early church—in their meetings and in their communities. Most of us are familiar with the account of the healing of the lame beggar outside the temple. Consider Peter's preaching to the multitudes after the miracle and the persecution which followed. You will quickly realize that he was not a seeker-friendly preacher, but you will have to admit that the results of his style of preaching were more impressive than anything you have seen in the seeker-friendly sanctuaries of America:

> Then Peter said, "Silver or gold I do not have, but what I do have I give you. In the name of Jesus Christ of Nazareth, walk." Taking him by the right hand, he helped him up, and instantly the man's feet and ankles became strong. He jumped to his feet and began to walk. Then he went with them into the temple courts, walking and jumping, and praising God. When all the people saw him walking and praising God, they recognized him as the same man who used to sit begging at the temple gate called Beautiful, and they were filled with wonder and amazement at what had happened to him. While the man held on to Peter and John, all the people were astonished and came running to them in the

> place called Solomon's Colonnade. When Peter saw this, he said to them: "Fellow Israelites, why does this surprise you? Why do you stare at us as if by our own power or godliness we had made this man walk? The God of Abraham, Isaac and Jacob, the God of our fathers, has glorified his servant Jesus. You handed him over to be killed, and you disowned him before Pilate, though he had decided to let him go. You disowned the Holy and Righteous One and asked that a murderer be released to you. You killed the author of life, but God raised him from the dead. We are witnesses of this. By faith in the name of Jesus, this man whom you see and know was made strong. It is Jesus' name and the faith that comes through him that has completely healed him, as you can all see."
>
> —Acts 3:6–16

The modern seeker-friendly gospel seems anemic alongside Peter's powerful confrontational preaching. But this is the style of evangelism you find throughout the early days of the church. Revolution, revival, exponential growth, and great excitement were the results. The demise of the church actually began when it became more popular and culture-current. It began its journey into delusion and declension when Constantine started promoting Christianity and erecting beautiful buildings for its followers. But let's stay focused for a moment on the glory days when power evangelism was still chosen over a more seeker-sensitive brand. Let's read the following verses with this question in mind: What good is relevance without power?

> The priests and the captain of the temple guard and the Sadducees came up to Peter and John while they were speaking to the people. They were greatly disturbed because the apostles were teaching the people, proclaiming in Jesus the resurrection of the dead. They seized Peter and John and, because it was evening, they put them in jail until the next day. But many who heard the message believed; so the number of men who believed grew to about five thousand. The next day the rulers, the elders and the teachers of the law met in Jerusalem. Annas the high priest was there, and so were Caiaphas, John, Alexander and others of the high priest's family. They had Peter and John brought before them and began to question them: "By what power or what name did you do this?" Then Peter, filled with the Holy Spirit, said to them: "Rulers and elders of the people! If we are being called to account today for an act of kindness shown to a man who was lame and are being asked how he was healed, then know this, you and all the people of Israel: It is by the name of Jesus Christ of Nazareth, whom you crucified but whom God raised from the dead, that this man stands before you healed.
> —Acts 4:1–10

We don't experience this kind of excitement in the seeker-sensitive sanctuaries of the church in America. We have sacrificed power on the altars of relevance. The early church experienced both excitement and power. The disciples refused to back up for the devil or water down their message for hypocritical religious leaders. Wherever they preached, miracles occurred and riot or revival broke out. The church experienced continual growth. They responded to threats and persecution by praying more fervently and preaching more passionately. Why would we want to trade that kind of excitement and power for a watered down seeker-friendly gospel with its superficial success?

It should be evident by now that two ingredients found everywhere in the early church are missing today: boldness and power. Consider how those early believers responded to threats, beatings, and imprisonment:

> "Now, Lord, consider their threats and enable your servants to speak your word with great boldness. Stretch out your hand to heal and perform signs and wonders through the name of your holy servant Jesus." After they prayed, the place where they were meeting was shaken. And they were all filled with the Holy Spirit and spoke the word of God boldly.
> —Acts 4:29–31

The early church continued to grow, but their approach never became seeker-friendly. After Ananias and Sapphira lied to the Holy Ghost and fell dead in a meeting, the Bible tells us that fear came on the people (Acts 5:1–11). In that threatening, uncomfortable atmosphere, reverence for the moving of the Holy Spirit was esteemed and growth continued.

> The apostles performed many signs and wonders among the people. And all the believers used to meet together in Solomon's Colonnade. No one else dared join them, even though they were highly regarded by the people. Nevertheless, more and more men and women believed in the Lord and were added to their number. As a result, people brought the sick

into the streets and laid them on beds and mats so that at least Peter's shadow might fall on some of them as he passed by. Crowds gathered also from the towns around Jerusalem, bringing their sick and those tormented by impure spirits, and all of them were healed.

—Acts 5:12–16

Such accounts of confrontational, power evangelism run straight through the Book of Acts. It bears no resemblance to the feeble evangelistic programs in the churches of America today. I don't think anyone who reads the Book of Acts would argue that we have not lost something. The question is, upon realizing our loss, what is the proper response? Should we continue conducting surveys and developing programs to appeal to the unchurched, or should we return to the philosophy and methods of the New Testament church?

Do we need more surveys, programs, and fresh ideas; or do we need to return to our roots and seek a fresh baptism of the Holy Spirit? Do we need to be cool, casual, and culture-current; or do we need more prayer, power, and passion? Your answers to these questions will depend on how you answer the following question. Which church was most effective: the New Testament church or the modern, seeker-friendly one? If your answer is the former, I challenge you to join me in renewed pursuit of the power of the Holy Spirit and the boldness which accompanies the power. Why don't we try Pentecost one more time?

Chapter 5

THE RETURN OF CHEAP GRACE

THE APOSTLE PAUL opposed anything that frustrated the grace of God. He considered both legalism and liberalism to be dangerous.¹ One produces narrow-mindedness and bondage; the other produces open-mindedness and liberty—liberty that goes beyond Scripture; liberty that leads to a casual attitude toward sin. Paul was all over both extremes in his writings. We would be wise to evaluate the current grace teachings in light of his revelation. It might also be helpful to revisit the writings of German theologian, Dietrich Bonheoffer, who was martyred by the Nazi's in 1945. He wrote the classic *The Cost of Discipleship* in which he raised the subject of cheap grace.² In God's providence, it survived the Nazi book burnings and has been circulated throughout the world. The grace message which has become so popular today was condemned by this great hero of the faith, just as it was by the Apostle Paul.

What is Bonheoffer's concept of cheap grace? It is grace that offers forgiveness without repentance. It is grace that embraces discipleship without cost. It is Christianity without commitment or a cross. It is the same grace being peddled by some of the most famous, most popular preachers of our day. It is cheap, but their tastes are not. Scratching itching ears is making them rich. The *new* grace revelation is actually as old as the first century; it floated then under a heresy called antinomianism.[3] The old heresy has risen from the dead and is being propagated by some of the most famous preachers on television today. The leaders of the Word of Faith movement are among them. Soon we will not just have another aberration of the gospel; we will have a mutation of cheap grace and perverted faith.

I saw the trend taking shape early on. I told my son some time ago, after a service with him at the Grace Center in Festus, Missouri, that it was just a matter of time until faith preachers would be preaching grace like it was their newest revelation. He laughed, "No way, Dad." He called me the following morning and said, "You are a prophet. They are already doing it. I just heard "Mr. Faith Man" preach grace like it was the greatest thing since custom made jets."

It is not hard to understand why so many are joining the parade. People eventually get tired of the same old perversion. The old dogs realize that you have to come up with new tricks now and then—even if you have to borrow them from somebody a little fresher than you and peddle them as if they were your own. Anyone who knows the Bible should understand how the game works. Paul made it clear that many Christians are gullible and short on discernment. They will go whichever way the wind is blowing. He referred to them as "infants, tossed back and forth by the waves, and blown here and there by every wind of teaching and by the cunning and craftiness of people in their deceitful scheming (Eph. 4:14).

The day will come when many of these gullible Christians get past the infancy stage and then the deceitful schemers will lose a lot of support. When that happens, they won't be able to feed the "ministry monsters"[4] they have created and there will be implosions everywhere. Huge ministries will begin to cave in on themselves and everyone—even the wind-tossed babies—will wake up. But that day isn't here yet, so those who see clearly must continue to sound warnings, even if for the moment they seem to fall on deaf ears. Mark it down; the modern message of the grace revolution is Dietrich Bonheoffer's cheap grace repackaged. Cool preachers in skinny jeans and leather jackets are peddling it, and everybody knows that *cool* sells.

I became concerned when I realized just how dangerous this new twist could be. I was talking to a veteran preacher recently who said without blinking, "You know the law has been done away, don't you?" I responded, "What do you mean by the law?" He answered without hesitation, "The law, the Ten Commandments." He then referred to Hebrews 7:12, 18–19: "For when the priesthood is changed, the law must be changed also.... The former regulation is set aside because it was weak and useless (for the law made nothing perfect), and a better hope is introduced, by which we draw near to God." He went on to quote Romans 6:14, "For sin shall no longer be your master, because you are not under the law, but under grace."

When I told him that he was mistaken and that the Ten Commandments would never be done away with, a heated discussion followed. I did my best to explain that the law of the Lord is perfect (Ps. 19:7) and that the Ten Commandments would be in force forever. He was shocked that I had not bought into the *new* revelation on grace. I told him that I was doing fine with the one I got from Jesus and Paul. I explained that the Levitical law with all its ritual, ceremony, and daily sacrifice had indeed been done away with; but not the Ten Commandments. Jesus said, "Do not think that I have come to abolish the Law or the Prophets; I have not come to abolish them but to fulfill them" (Matt. 5:17). The Law was not done away with under the covenant of grace; it was written on our hearts. It became internal, rather than external.

Here's the good news of grace under the new and better covenant: If we mess up and sin, the law cannot condemn us because Jesus has already suffered and paid the penalty of sin for us. We repent, confess our sin, and receive forgiveness by faith. There is no need to do away with the Law. We simply live by a higher law under the covenant of grace: the law of the Spirit of life in Christ Jesus (Rom. 8:2). How can anyone who knows the Word say that the law has been abolished when the Bible clearly teaches that it has been written on our hearts: "This is the covenant that I will make with them after those days, saith the Lord, I will put my laws into their hearts, and in their minds will I write them;" (Heb. 10:16, KJV).

Why do so many want to do away with the law? Could it be that modern Christians are trying to find a cheap imitation of grace that comes with a license to sin? The law has not been abolished. It has just been transferred from the external realm of fleshly effort to the internal realm of spiritual power. What could not be accomplished through fleshly efforts to conform to an external code of conduct can now be realized through dependence on the power of the internal Spirit.

To take grace to the extreme of doing away with the law is to return to the first century heresy mentioned earlier: Antinomianism, which means against law. The true Christian who is under grace is not against law. He doesn't want to do away with it. He simply understands that the way to keep it is from an internal desire toward morality that is empowered by grace, not by an external compulsion that labors to keep it by human effort or will.

Consider what Paul said about the cheap grace that people want to use as a license to sin:

> The law was brought in so that the trespass might increase. But where sin increased, grace increased all the more, so that, just as sin reigned in death, so also grace might reign through righteousness to bring eternal life through Jesus Christ our Lord.... What shall we say, then? Shall we go on sinning so that grace may increase? By no means! We are those who have died to sin; how can we live in it any longer.
> —ROMANS 5:20–21; 6:1–2

He also dealt with this danger in Galatians. Paul understood that liberalism with its license to sin was just as dangerous as legalism with its demands of external conformity to the law. He stressed in his Epistle to the Galatians that we have been redeemed from the curse of the law; but he also warned against the excesses of grace induced liberty:

> Stand fast therefore in the liberty wherewith Christ hath made us free, and be not entangled again with the yoke of bondage.... For, brethren, ye have been called unto liberty; only use not liberty for an occasion to the flesh, but by love serve one another. For all the law is fulfilled in one word, even in this; Thou shalt love thy neighbour as thyself.
> —Galatians 5:1, 13–14, kjv

We know that one aspect of grace is God's favor, mercy, and love being poured out on people who don't deserve it. I have often heard it explained with this acrostic: "God's Riches At Christ's Expense." Grace is freely given. We can do nothing to deserve or earn it.

> That in the ages to come he might shew the exceeding riches of his grace in his kindness toward us through Christ Jesus. For by grace are ye saved through faith; and that not of yourselves: it is the gift of God: Not of works, lest any man should boast.
> —Ephesians 2:7–9, kjv

But there is another side of grace. It is not the cheap grace which gives its recipients a license to sin without retribution. It is not grace that caters to the desires of the flesh without fear of negative consequences. It is not forgiveness without repentance. Paul said, "Use not liberty for an occasion to the flesh" (Gal. 5:13, kjv). In other words, don't be deceived into thinking that your new freedom in grace gives you liberty to do whatever you want to do without repercussions. There is another side of grace that we must consider. It is found in Titus 2:11–14:

The Return of Cheap Grace

> For the grace of God has appeared that offers salvation to all people. It teaches us to say "No" to ungodliness and worldly passions, and to live self-controlled, upright and godly lives in this present age, while we wait for the blessed hope—the appearing of the glory of our great God and Savior, Jesus Christ, who gave himself for us to redeem us from all wickedness and to purify for himself a people that are his very own, eager to do what is good.

This is not the cheap grace that wants to do away with the law. This is grace that gives strength to do what human effort failed to do—keep the law by the power of the Spirit. If we fail, we are not condemned. We repent and receive mercy and appropriate forgiveness. This is the grace of God. This is not grace that finds ways to indulge the flesh and justify pursuing the pleasures of this world. This is grace that teaches us to turn from sin and live righteous lives to the glory of God. It requires something of us, but it freely gives us all that is needed to meet the requirements. This is more than God's undeserved love, mercy, and favor. This aspect of grace is God's strength and ability which enable us to please Him and do His will. Paul is not adding works as a requirement to salvation. This is not grace and works; it is grace that works.

> For I am the least of the apostles and do not even deserve to be called an apostle, because I persecuted the church of God. But by the grace of God I am what I am, and his grace to me was not without effect. No, I worked harder than all of them—yet not I, but the grace of God that was with me.
> —1 Corinthians 15:9–10

True grace does not seek ways to exempt itself from the law. It doesn't want to do away with the law. That is the effort of cheap grace which desires gratification of self more than it desires to please God. True grace loves the law. It desires to keep it by the power of the Spirit. It rejoices that we have been delivered from the curse of the law and rejoices that now we have received power to keep the law that has been written on our hearts. Cheap grace draws people down a destructive path of carelessness and compromise. The true grace of God which teaches us to deny what others allow takes us up another pathway—a pathway that leads to the glorious liberty of the sons of God (Rom. 8:21). This is the true grace of God that reigns in life.

> For if, by the trespass of the one man, death reigned through that one man, how much more will those who receive God's abundant provision of grace and of the gift of righteousness reign in life through the one man, Jesus Christ!...The law was brought in so that the trespass might increase. But where sin increased, grace increased all the more, so that, just as sin reigned in death, so also grace might reign through righteousness to bring eternal life through Jesus Christ our Lord.
> —ROMANS 5:17, 20–21

True grace has no desire to play games with sin. It is not looking for exemptions which allow the flesh to indulge in ungodly living. It says "No" to ungodliness and turns from sin. It has a made up mind which is resolved to please God. There is nothing cheap about it. True grace is free; but it cost Jesus dearly to be able to offer it freely. Cheap grace is for spiritual infants, game players, and pretenders. Costly grace freely given is for the spiritually mature who have exercised their senses to be able to discern between good and evil (Heb. 5:13–14). Costly grace is embraced by those who appreciate it because they know it was bought for us at a great price: the blood of Jesus. It is free but it is not cheap. Jesus paid for it with blood. Grace bought with sinless blood should never be lightly esteemed or carelessly used to justify sin. It is given to the end that we might conquer sin on the battlefield of life, not so we can play with it in a sandbox on some religious playground.

Grace that leads to lawlessness is not true grace. It is a counterfeit; it is a delusion. Grace that leads to ungodliness and allows indulgence in worldly lusts is not true grace. It is a seducing misrepresentation; it is a perverted distortion of something precious and holy. The Bible warns us to beware of those who pervert the grace of God. Perhaps we should listen to purveyors of cheap grace with a bit more caution and a lot more discernment—or perhaps we shouldn't listen to them at all.

> Dear friends, although I was very eager to write to you about the salvation we share, I felt compelled to write and urge you to contend for the faith that was once for all entrusted to God's holy people. For certain individuals whose condemnation was written about long ago have secretly slipped in among you. They are ungodly people, who pervert the grace of our God into a license for immorality and deny Jesus Christ our only Sovereign and Lord.
> —Jude 1:3–4

Who are those who pervert the grace of God? They are those who carry it to such extremes that it leaves people with the idea that it is a license for immorality. You may never hear them deny Jesus with their words as Jude suggests, but they deny Him just the same; they deny Him by using a misrepresentation of grace to justify an immoral lifestyle. It is dangerous to emphasize one truth to the neglect of others. It always creates an imbalance, which can lead to deception and full-blown heresy. We must guard our hearts against deception.

We are living in the last days; and just as John warned, many false prophets have gone out into the world (1 John 4:1). Our greatest safeguard against deception is to become grounded in the Word and rely on the anointing of the Holy Spirit to help us exercise our senses to discern between good and evil. This book began with Paul's words in 1 Timothy 4:1. I hope they will now carry more weight as I repeat them here: "The Spirit clearly says that in later times some will abandon the faith and follow deceiving spirits and things taught by demons."

May we never succumb to the seduction of the deceivers with their doctrines of demons. May we rather live with confidence in the Word and the Spirit and give our hearts fully "to him who is able to keep you from stumbling and to present you before his glorious presence without fault and with great joy—to the only God our Savior be glory, majesty, power and authority, through Jesus Christ our Lord, before all ages, now and forevermore! Amen" (Jude 1:24–25).

And, may we always welcome the true grace of God—the kind that causes us to live with reverence and godly fear:

Therefore, since we are receiving a kingdom which cannot be shaken, let us have grace, by which we may serve God acceptably with reverence and godly fear. For our God is a consuming fire.
—Hebrews 12:28–29, NKJV

Chapter 6

LYING SIGNS AND WONDERS

And many false prophets will appear and will deceive many people.... False prophets will rise up and perform great signs and wonders so as to deceive, if possible, even God's chosen ones.
—Matthew 24:11, 24, NLT

The coming of the lawless one is according to the working of Satan, with all power, signs, and lying wonders, and with all unrighteous deception among those who perish, because they did not receive the love of the truth, that they might be saved.
—2 Thessalonians 2:9–10, NKJV

I BECAME DEEPLY CONCERNED for the church in America after years of missionary work in different nations. While recovering from malaria, which I contracted in Mali, West Africa, I was "blessed" with some down time. I spent a good amount of it doing something I had seldom done—watching Christian television. I was shocked at what I saw and heard. I listened to false doctrine, stared in disbelief as preachers sold miracles and urged viewers to sow a financial seed for a miracle harvest, and I watched famous televangelists manipulate crowds and their viewers with "miracles" that didn't happen. I realized that I was seeing the fulfillment of Jesus' warnings concerning the last days. And I understood that "lying signs and wonders" were all over Christian television in America. I concluded that America needed missionaries as much as Africa. And that is when I got serious about writing a few more books.

I have been accused, by some who read my previous books of making things worse by challenging deceivers and drawing attention to doctrines of demons and the work of seducing spirits. I maintain that I am on solid ground and in the presence of good company: Peter, Paul, Jude, and John did the same thing. I am compelled to raise the issues that fill these pages. I have been told by some pastors, who no longer invite me to speak at their churches, that people in the world don't need to hear about these things. I wonder, where have they been? Have they heard of Facebook, the Internet, and YouTube? Trust me, the world knows. Non-Christians watch the foolishness of charismatic leaders and the craziness that takes place in their meetings for entertainment.

The leaders I describe in these pages have brought so much reproach on the church it's a wonder that anybody listens to what any of us has to say. The world no longer holds much respect for the church, and unscrupulous leaders own a lot of the blame for that. We will never recover the respect of the lost unless we are willing to confront evil and falsehood in the church. Far from turning unbelievers off, I think many will be relieved when they see leaders confronting deceivers and thereby sending a message that says, "We are not all like this." The world interprets our silence as acceptance. That being said, I am going to dive into deeper waters.

What are lying signs and wonders? They are often counterfeit or concocted miracles performed by false prophets. Sometimes they are just natural phenomena akin to sleight of hand tricks employed by magicians. Sometimes they are actual supernatural manifestations; but Satan, not God, is their source. He uses them to deceive and to confirm the already deceived in error and delusion. The Bible has a lot to say about lying signs and wonders and the false prophets who produce them. It warns believers to be on guard against them, especially in the last days. Deception is dangerous; the New Testament is filled with warnings to alert us to the danger.

The wonder to me is that people are actually duped by the lying signs and wonders manufactured by these modern deceivers. The present concocters of lying sign and wonders are lightweights compared to those we will meet just a little farther up the road. Hindu holy men and witchdoctors have for a long time been producing much more impressive ones than those we have seen in the charismatic church lately. The failure of Spirit-filled Christians to discern what is happening should be of great concern to those who see it for what it is. It must be a strong delusion.

It is due in part to the reticence of leaders who are not deceived yet refuse to raise their voices against it.

These leaders know clearly what is going on but they won't open their mouths for fear of being accused of judging or touching "God's anointed." The thought of a little controversy or rejection sends them to the corner to sit down in silence. We need some preachers who haven't sunk to their knees in surrender to politeness and political correctness. What is polite about not warning the gullible that there are wolves dressed in sheep's clothing in front of cameras, behind pulpits, and on platforms all across America? The Apostle Paul and the leaders of the early church didn't let fear of reprisal or rejection shut them up. In fact, they kept preaching truth boldly in the face of persecution, prison, and even death. They feared not to call deceiving prophets by their first name—False.

I believe in bona fide miracles. I have personally experienced several miraculous healings. The meaning of *bona fide* is pertinent to the subject matter in this chapter. Most people realize that it conveys the idea of being authentic or genuine. It also means "without deception or fraud."[1] Unfortunately, there are many pretenders today who lack character; the miracles they claim to produce are as false as they themselves are. They operate like the lawless one described in the verses we read at the beginning of this chapter. Any serious student of Scripture who is not asleep at the wheel should realize that the church has suffered an infestation of false prophets—"propheliars," I call them. I have never understood why many believers find it so difficult to believe that some preachers are not what they appear to be. They manufacture miracles—or simply make it appear that a miracle has taken place when it has not—and wonder of wonders, they keep getting away with the same old tricks.

These "propheliars" are experts at trafficking in lying signs and wonders. A number of televangelists and crusade preachers have developed it into a fine art and have prospered greatly through their cunning. These men are not truthful and the miracles they produce are not genuine. They do it because money follows miracles—even staged ones. Vulnerable people are easily conned into giving when they think a miracle has occurred.

It is sad that only a few of the pastors and leaders who know what is taking place are willing to address it. Most fear that questioning famous preachers will cause too much controversy; they don't want to risk being thought negative or critical, they don't want to be accused of touching "God's anointed." So, the honest leaders remain silent and the deceivers get louder.

A favorite tactic of some manufacturers of miracles and "lying signs and wonders" has for years involved the distribution and collection of prayer cards. Even the "little shots" can pull this one off. People are asked before, or at the beginning of the service, to write their names and addresses on the prayer cards. The sick are asked to write a detailed description of their sickness. The cards are then used to produce "words of knowledge."

Not everyone is as sophisticated with it as a couple of "evangelists" have been. They are wired, or wireless these days, to an assistant behind the platform or backstage. When it comes time to dispense the "words of knowledge" the "evangelist" mysteriously hears a voice in his ear; it is the voice of his assistant, who is often someone like his wife or brother-in-law, reading from prayer cards. The unwary sick in the crowd are amazed that the great "evangelist" not only gets a revelation of the specifics of their sickness, but he even hears God tell him where they live. Gullible people think: "It's supernatural!" But some of us haven't fallen asleep at the wheel and we know much of what is called supernatural these days is actually "superfabricated." I am saddened to have to inform people who desperately need a miracle that some rich preachers are not above such shameful and deceptive behavior. It should not be a surprise to them, but it almost always is. I sometimes wonder if anybody really believes what Jesus and the apostles said about the proliferation of false prophets and seducing spirits in the last days.

Another favorite tactic of unscrupulous crusade evangelists is to get someone out of a wheelchair and get him to take a few steps. When they do, the music often gets louder, the lights get brighter, and the famous evangelist gets more animated—all to the delight of the gullible crowd. It's often all a lie. The evangelist doesn't tell the crowd that the person was able to take a few steps before being prayed for—many people in wheelchairs can walk, just not very far. But the emotional crowd, caught up in the excitement of the artificial atmosphere, just doesn't get it. The masterful deceiver knows how it works and takes full advantage of the unwary, unthinking crowd.

When the person gets out of the wheelchair and takes a few steps, ushers or armor bearers quickly come along beside him. The evangelist springs into action and a solid line of singers and ushers quickly line up shoulder to shoulder on each side of him. This serves to block the crowd's view of the person with the wheelchair. While the evangelist is still proclaiming the great miracle, the man slumps back down into the wheelchair and ushers quickly take him off the platform: if the crusade preacher has much money at all, he might have a more sophisticated platform—one with a ramp at the back, out of view of the crowd. The man was not healed; but the crowd, worked into frenzy by this point, thinks he was. They don't see him sitting behind the big platform wondering why the ushers don't push him back into the crowd. It is all a lie—and it is a wonder that people fall for it—but they do; and some modern false prophets can pull it (and variations of it) off without a hitch.

I don't understand why the honest preachers, who know what is going on, remain silent. Most nonbelievers recognize the falsehood and fakery for what it is and laugh at the Christians who don't. They must wonder why more Christian leaders don't publicly confront and condemn such reprehensible conduct. I wonder with them. Our silence speaks loudly to a watching world—a world that concludes: if other Christian leaders won't speak against it they must all be in bed together.

Let me temper this assault on the false by saying that I believe in miracles. I have personally experienced and seen numerous authentic healings. I am not a cynic. I have absolutely no doubt that "Jesus Christ is the same yesterday and today and forever" (Heb. 13:8) and that He is still performing miracles. But I am not naive. I realize that there are many deceivers who are masters at manipulating crowds with false claims. We should be on guard, and we should warn people about these charlatans. Have you ever noticed how many of the claims of miracles by televangelists are constantly things the eye can't see? And there is seldom, if ever, medical verification. People get healed of headaches, backaches, stomach aches, hearing problems, etc., and testify of their healing. People who faint or pass out are declared dead by a deceiver with no medical background. The "great man of God" prays and when his victim wakes up, he claims that Jesus raised him from the dead. There is no medical verification that he was actually dead but the crowd goes along with it. After the "resurrection" the evangelist helps his victim with leading questions in order to embellish his testimony for the crowd. By the time it is reported in a newsletter, the man has died, gone to heaven, and returned to tell everybody about the great miracle. The guy sometimes goes along with it because he is manipulated by the persuasive evangelist. Others go along with the charade because they like the attention and the thrill of standing before a large crowd. Sometimes it even gets him a token offering from the manipulating evangelist. It's a wonder he doesn't come back reporting that Jesus told him that everyone should sow a thousand dollar resurrection seed into the ministry of the "great evangelist." Wait a minute; I think that they have already done that—more than once.

    Forgive me for being underwhelmed and a bit sarcastic, but it is beyond ridiculous. I know firsthand of an evangelist who prayed for a passed out drunk that came back to the land of the living. By the next meeting, the drunk had allegedly died and had no pulse for several minutes. Can you believe that people buy stories like that? The profits are good when you can sell something you got for free. But when preachers who have maligned and misused the gospel answer to the One who gave it, I have no doubt that they will deeply regret their deceptive and fraudulent practices.

The most masterful manipulators understand a little about the psychology of human behavior. They know that most insecure people will agree with an authority figure or try to say or do what they think he wants. I have been at meetings where all sorts of testimonies of invisible miracles were reported, while other people with very visible problems left just as they came—blind, in wheel chairs, or on crutches. One would think that with so many claims of healing you would see more of the visible ailments healed also. The sad truth is: there are a lot of deceivers who manufacture miracles in order to manipulate a crowd. They know that money follows miracles, even conjured up ones.

I have been criticized for bringing these things to light. Believers have accused me of discrediting the gospel before the unbelieving. Tell that to the true prophets and preachers of the Bible. They exposed everything that was false at every opportunity. Unbelievers may actually start believing that some of us still have credibility if they hear us exposing fraud and confronting deceivers. The only reason I am reticent to discuss these issues is because I don't want to take anything away from genuine faith. Authentic healings and miracles still occur. I testify of them at every opportunity. But I also want to warn people to be on guard against the fraudsters who traffic in fake ones. We need discernment. Jesus said, "Many false prophets will appear and deceive many people"

(Matt. 24:11). In his first Epistle, John emphasizes our need for discernment: "Dear friends, do not believe every spirit, but test the spirits to see whether they are from God, because many false prophets have gone out into the world" (1 John 4:1).

Did you notice that both Jesus and John used the word *many* in these verses? Jesus used it twice and John once. The meaning is clear: there are a lot of deceivers around today. We desperately need discernment to recognize the counterfeits and expose false prophets who prey on vulnerable people. Here's how the *God's Word* translation renders 1 John 4:1: "Dear friends, don't believe all people who say that they have the Spirit. Instead, test them. See whether the spirit they have is from God, because there are many false prophets in the world."

Jesus is still performing miracles today. What He did while on earth in a human body, He is doing today through His spiritual body, the church. The Bible says He is "the same yesterday and today and forever" (Heb. 13:8). I have both seen and personally experienced the miracles that Jesus still performs. I encourage people to pray for miracles and believe God for healing. But I don't want people to be naïve and fall victim to the deceivers.

I loved Kathryn Kuhlman's crusades. She put on a bit of a show, but there was a major difference between her and those who imitate her today—real miracles occurred in her meetings. She was an intriguing, charismatic person who knew how to get a crowd excited; but she didn't resort to the shameless exaggeration and hype of modern televangelists, manufacturers of miracles, and makers of movements. She didn't have to; real miracles—visible ones—took place in her meetings and they created enough excitement all by themselves. There was no doubt that God's power was manifest. That's why so many have tried to imitate her. Several have succeeded in mastering some of her vocal intonations and mannerisms—including a former friend of mine who studied her for years. But none of the imitators have succeeded in moving in the anointing or reproducing the power that operated in her meetings.

She was different than the "magicians" who pull miracles out of a "haze" to manipulate crowds today. She often had medical doctors present to add credence to claims of healing. She encouraged people to follow up with testing by their doctors. Claims of healing by televangelists today have often been exposed as false when it was discovered that the person who allegedly experienced a miracle actually did not. Grandiose claims vaporize under the heat of the slightest scrutiny. A famous televangelist, who continually claims that many incredible healings take place in his crusades, was not able to produce verifiable evidence for even one of them when he was challenged by a well-known, evangelical radio personality. His experience has been oft repeated with lesser known evangelists who fell into the hands of investigative journalists who knew their trade.

Most people have become aware of scandals involving money when phony preachers were exposed for moral misconduct in reports of investigative journalists. Credible leaders in the Charismatic movement should be confronting the phonies before the Bible Answer Man or secular journalists have a chance to. They bring reproach on all of us. We should be exposing those who refuse to repent before the media does. Charismatic leaders need to recover the lost art of confrontation. False prophets and immoral televangelists should not be allowed to go on unchallenged. We need to begin policing ourselves.

There is a tragic mixture of truth and falsehood in modern movements. Sometimes when the deception of a famous evangelist is revealed, the false gets more publicity and the authentic is questioned. In the face of suspicion, we need to testify even more about authentic and verifiable miracles—past and present. It is difficult to write material like this because, while I want to expose the false, I don't want to discourage anyone from believing that genuine miracles still occur. That's why I am writing another book entitled *Miles of Miracles*. It is an account of miraculous healing and deliverance from my evangelistic and missionary ministry around the world, including some I have experienced personally. Miracles still happen. I urge you: Don't let the counterfeit rob you of faith to believe for the authentic. You don't stop using money because there are counterfeit bills in the mix. Don't stop using faith to believe for authentic miracles because there are counterfeit ones taking place.

Today the charismatic church is filled with pretenders and imitators. I wouldn't want the job of counting all the healing evangelists who have studied Kathryn Kuhlman in order to copy her methods and style. Imitations are just that. What imitators produce is usually a lot like what they are. You would think that preachers who know the Word would remember the seven sons of Sceva who tried to imitate Paul in Acts 19. They talked like him, acted like him, and said the same words that he said—but they didn't

Lying Signs and Wonders

get the results he did. Paul's words were weighted with authority and power; the words of the imitators were as light as feathers. The demons respected Paul, but not his imitators. They were embarrassed when they were beaten and stripped by a demon possessed man who chased them down the street screaming: We know Jesus and we know Paul; but who are you? (Acts 19:15–16).

People desperate to see the supernatural often willingly cooperate with manipulating preachers and act like something happened when they know it didn't. Insecure people are sometimes overwhelmed when they find themselves standing in front of a crowd. They will do and say just about anything they think the leader wants them to. When he lays hands on them and pushes, they give him a courtesy drop whether they feel the power of God or not. Others get the idea and follow suit. Soon people are laying everywhere on the floor. Does the power of God operate in meetings where people are pushed down or donate "courtesy drops?" If that is not authentic, then what else is not authentic? Are the personal prophecies given by such men to be trusted? Lying signs and wonders are everywhere. It gives one pause to think what will happen when false prophets operating under a stronger demonic anointing produce more dynamic lying signs and wonders. How many ingenuous believers will be so impressed that they quickly sacrifice truth on the altar of a false supernatural experience?

It requires discernment to separate the true from the false. The airwaves and convention centers of America are filled with con men who know how to work a crowd. Miracles are staged and multitudes think they are real.

Why do these shameless deceivers resort to such tactics? It's all about the money. Miracles—even phony ones—always result in bigger offerings. The devil will help a deceiver raise offerings as long as he is willing to sell his soul. The warnings of Jesus often seem to have fallen on deaf ears. It never enters the mind of many Christians that false prophets are doing just what He said they would. People fall for the same old tricks—over and over again.

In the 1980s a false prophetess burst on the scene and quickly became famous in charismatic circles because well-known leaders were quick to promote her. Oil oozed out of her fingertips, "blood" appeared on her palms, and "dove" feathers and diamonds began falling out of thin air as she pranced around on the stage and prayed for people. But the main event was always the offering. Well-known leaders, pastors, and evangelists were warned by people who claimed she was a phony who practiced witchcraft. Some even produced evidence that she was a deceiver who had done the same things before. But a long list of famous leaders ignored the warnings.

The crowds were big and the offerings were huge. Some concluded that was the reason several big name pastors and leaders in the word of faith and seed faith worlds continued promoting her and inviting her to speak at their conferences and churches—even after the evidence was on the table. People were often told to bring their offerings as gold dust, dove feathers, or diamonds began to appear—or when the oil began to flow. They were deceived into thinking healings occurred simultaneously with the manifestations, and the excitement grew at just the right time: gullible believers lined up to take offerings up front where the anointing was. One of the blessings extended to those who sowed generous financial seeds was the privilege of picking up a prayer cloth after they deposited their gifts.

It is amazing how weirdness seems to attract people who can't wait to give away large sums of hard earned money. It is even more amazing to me that people are so easily deceived by such trickery. A new crop of false prophets is still deceiving the gullible with the same old tricks years after she was exposed.

I was aware that such things had been going on in various parts of Latin America for many years. Stigmata were common among Catholics, not only in Latin America but other parts of the world. Corrupt priests used vials of "blood" to trick the superstitious. They did it for the same reason big names in America promoted this false prophetess: crowds and money follow miracles—even conjured up ones.

I clashed with men using a young woman with a familiar spirit, much like the slave girl out of whom Paul cast a demon in Acts 16, in a square in front of a Catholic church in Bogota, Columbia, in 1975. I was amazed to see hundreds gather in a matter of about fifteen minutes as the young woman worked the crowd telling people personal things about themselves or their families—things that she had no way of knowing. Containers quickly filled with money. This sort of thing was not at all uncommon in cities throughout Mexico and Latin America. When I started distributing Spanish gospel tracts and preaching to the crowd, the girl was distracted. She kept "missing it" and people laughed and began to leave. Her spell over the crowd was broken.

Remembering Paul's experience in Acts 16, I surveyed the crowd looking for those she worked for. Two men in expensive suits were already coming toward me. They shoved people out of the way as they struggled to get to where I stood on the other side of the crowd. I escaped by merging with people as they scattered. I outran the fat guys in expensive suits. They stopped outside my hotel as I asked the clerk at the front desk to call the police and report that two thugs had chased me up the street.

Upon returning to the USA, I was not surprised to see things I had witnessed in Latin America taking place here—but I was surprised to see that so many educated adults were being deceived by them. Charismatic churches are filled with unwary people who are easily deceived because they so desperately want to see supernatural manifestations. Today I think many charismatics are looking more for supernatural manifestations than they are for the "Manifester." That is why we need more real shepherds, not more self-appointed apostles and prophets.

Among the numerous people who told the big name preachers promoting this woman that it was trickery was a young preacher in Tulsa. He knew that the dove feathers weren't falling out of thin air. And careful observation revealed that many instances of oil and "blood" appearing on the hands of deceivers often comes from little vials that are squeezed at select moments. It is a cheap trick that has been used forever by witches, magicians, fighters, and unscrupulous priests and preachers. It shouldn't even require discernment to detect; but famous leaders in the Word of Faith and Charismatic movements were duped— or were they? It shook me to see how easy it was to deceive people. Why did famous leaders and pastors of big churches promote this woman? Surely they weren't duped by such simple tricks, were they?

Being familiar with some magic and sleight of hand tricks, the young preacher saw what others apparently didn't. Like me, he was appalled that famous leaders didn't see it (or didn't want to) and he became determined to convince them. It is hard to believe that leaders were so naïve. Cheap tricks used by deceivers have more than once been caught on camera. One man was so disgusted with the farce, and even more so that the most famous preachers were promoting it, that he gathered up some of the feathers left laying on the stage and had them analyzed at a lab. Would you believe it? They weren't dove feathers at all; they were dirty duck feathers.

Today we even have angel feathers falling! But it is so "old hat" and so overused now, I don't expect that anyone who still thinks and tries the spirits will bother to have any feathers analyzed. It doesn't seem to matter anyway. People just keep falling for the same old tricks. There must be some strong deluding demons and seducing spirits at work. I'm not interested in picking up any of the feathers, but I would like to sweep up some of the gold dust that is reportedly falling to have it analyzed. But it seems to vaporize as soon as the preacher announces its appearance. It would also be interesting to have the glitter that appears in "glory clouds" analyzed. I fear that the results would reveal that you can buy little plastic packages of the stuff at any Walmart. But it sure gets a crowd excited when the lights are directed at the "glory cloud" with gold dust glittering in it.

Do you ever wonder where will it all end? Why aren't more leaders finding their voices and attempting to bring the masses out of a deluded fog of "drunken glory?" Does "touch not God's anointed" really mean that we should just stand aside and let this foolishness continue unconfronted? There is so much falsehood and fakery it's exhausting to even try to write about it. Minimal research yields enough material to fill an encyclopedia. I am listing one reference, just in case you are curious. I really like the name of the site: *Redeemed Hippies' Place*. I like it because I am a redeemed hippie. That may be why all this weirdness doesn't attract me. I saw much stranger—and much more impressive—supernatural phenomena on acid trips with fellow hippies in Southern California a long time ago. The video posted by the *Redeemed Hippies' Place* includes manifestations like "diamonds" spilling out of a woman's mouth."[2] I wonder how they got there!

I remember one meeting where the crowd went wild when the speaker reported that gold dust was descending on the platform and asked them to bring their offerings as the "miracle was occurring." By squinting you could see dust particles catching the light of the sun. I have to admit though: they did have the glimmer of gold to them. The most bizarre memory I have of the gold fiascos is one of a famous evangelist explaining his theory in front of the cameras on a big Christian network. Something was causing vibrations in heaven—I think it may have been praise—and the dust was descending on us from the streets of gold.

The duck feathers I mentioned earlier were eventually discussed with some of the big name ministers who promoted the false prophetess. Their lack of discernment, or pretense, caused me to become a lot more cautious about who I listened to. Some of us thought the famous leaders who promoted her might make a statement, but as far as I know, they never did. The word on the street was that some knew all along that she was a deceiver. It is difficult to imagine how they could not have known. I was the champion of too many pillow fights with my little brothers to fall for the falling feathers; but famous leaders did—or did they?

I don't know. Maybe the big name leaders would have exposed her if it would not have made them appear so dishonest or deficient in discernment. They covered it up, swept the duck feathers, diamonds, and dirt under the rug, and she faded away when the big boys stopped promoting her—for awhile. The tarnished deceiver reappeared later to bamboozle a new crop of willing to be hoodwinked believers. Her comeback was aided by the prophetic head of a Christian TV network who also brought us some others of the same spirit. Thanks, man.

I could relate countless stories like this, and name numerous discredited prophets with whom I had some association, but I don't think it is necessary and I don't want to wear you out. Those who have discernment will have no difficulty believing what I have reported here, so I will stop with just one more account of "evangelastic" activity. I was one of the speakers at a conference during the gold dust and gold fillings era. I was shocked when attending a meeting led by another speaker to hear him announce that cavities were being filled and amalgam fillings were being replaced with gold. I later learned that he was a man who was determined to make a name for himself by reports of miraculous phenomena in his meetings.

My first thought when I heard his decree of what God was doing was: if God is going to go to all that trouble why doesn't He just replace the whole tooth? But no sooner had I thought it than a woman began crying out, "Oh, my God! Oh, my God!" (By the way: She and the evangelist were good friends.) The excited sister went on to say that God had just given her a gold filling. I wondered how she knew since she hadn't looked in a mirror, but evidently no one else was as cynical as I. The speaker asked another sister to check her teeth. She reported that she indeed had a gold filling. Forgive me for thinking that she had it before the meeting. I believe in miracles but not false ones. The crowd didn't share my skepticism. People went wild and many went to look in the mouth of a woman they didn't know! The kind of confusion and chaos Paul tried to curb in the Corinthian church took over the meeting. I watched in wonder and asked myself: Are we really this easily deceived?

Some of the things that took place in the 1970s and 1980s are child's play compared to what came later. The foolishness we allowed yesterday opened the door for the deception we are experiencing today. I have concerns that go much deeper than word of faith preachers and seed seekers trying to get my money, much deeper than confusion and division over bizarre manifestations brought about by manipulative leaders who dispense spiritual drunkenness: I am watching, with a wary eye, a group of leaders who I believe want to control everything. Their false humility does not impress me. What they are saying and doing makes the leaders of the Shepherding movement look like school boys. I believe the greatest danger facing the Charismatic movement is not leaders who encourage behaviors that make us look foolish; it is not the cons who want to deceive us and take our money. It is leaders who wear big titles and operate with illegitimate authority: my concern is that they don't just want to deceive us—they want to rule us. But few suspect it because all the little leaders with big titles have such pleasant personalities. False apostles and prophets couldn't be so nice, could they?

If you have read this far, you are probably someone who is already grieved over what is happening in the church in America today. The deceivers have become shameless. Some of the things I have described are now no more than minor league tricks. Deception has moved to the big leagues. We need to pray for greater discernment to return to the church—especially to the charismatic arm of it. The laughter outside is getting louder. The nonsensical behavior of charismatic leaders has stripped us of respect in the world's eyes.

False prophets have operated without being confronted or challenged for so long they are becoming more brazen by the moment. The fables are becoming more farfetched. Stories about rooms of spare body parts in heaven give gullible sign seekers goose bumps. The spare body parts people also claim that metal rods in peoples' bodies dissolve and are replaced by bone. They also claim restorative miracles like missing or malfunctioning body parts being restored. Had miracles like some of those described actually occurred, they would have been reported on news outlets around the world. It should be a simple matter to obtain medical verification for incredible miracles. If somebody got a new arm, I am certain they would want to go and witness to the doctor who had amputated it. His report would be interesting to read. I have contacted numerous ministries asking for verification of some of the more bizarre claims of miracles. I have been waiting a long time for a response.

Bizarre tales of traveling back through time and moving through different dimensions don't even cause undiscerning believers to ask, "Is there any suggestion of such a thing in the Bible?" All manner of New Age practices are common in the Charismatic movement today. Things I did, like channeling and soul travel, as a hippie using mind-altering drugs and studying Eastern mysticism are common in some charismatic circles today. A popular prophetess associated with the New Apostolic Reformation takes trips forward and backward through time on an angel that appears in the form of a big brown eagle. People listen in awe as she rehearses the story in meetings. The first time she returned from a trip on the angel-eagle, she claims that God gave her a confirmation to convince her that it was all real—there were brown feathers on her stairs and around her desk. Do angels really have feathers? Do they shed them?

A young woman the eagle flyer mentors takes trips to the third heaven on a regular basis—and makes it sound as easy as driving to Walmart to pick up a few groceries. She is also skilled at unwinding snakes from people's bodies, or pulling them out of their eyes, ears, and mouths and casting them into the abyss as she leads the lovers of myths in chants of "Burn! Burn! Burn!" I am a bit wary of that because witchdoctors in Africa are good at unwinding snakes. But I must say that I have never heard of one casting snakes into the abyss and crying, "Burn!"

I am not surprised that the stories become increasingly more bizarre. The Apostle Paul said that people who turn away from the truth would be attracted to teachers who are given to myths (2 Tim. 4:3–4). False prophets know that myths attract multitudes and money. Need I say more? Popular charismatic pastors, who seem to be linked to other marketers of myths, talk about glory clouds, gold dust, and feathers falling everywhere without cracking a smile—and the itching ears people love it. The fabricators of foolish fables and marketers of made-up myths are not really very convincing—at least to those who have developed their spiritual senses through diligent study and application of truth. But in today's charismatic circles, there always seems to be an abundance of sign seekers who are ready for a new story about something paranormal or extrabiblical that sounds remotely supernatural.

Doesn't anyone remember how shocked and disappointed everyone was years ago when the dove feathers that fell in meetings were analyzed as duck feathers? And aren't the gold dust stories getting a bit worn out too? And the glory clouds: I saw better ones at rock concerts in my hippie days. It is all so asinine; it saddens me that there is even a need to address it. There is delusion in the air at meetings where experience is exalted over truth. If you don't want to become one of the itching ears people who are fascinated by fables and mesmerized by myths, I encourage you to get back to the Bible. It is the greatest safeguard against deception.

Seducing spirits are defeated and driven out when they are forcefully confronted with the light of truth. Honest leaders who know we are in the midst of great deception and delusion need to find their voices. If we do not deal with the present darkness, something worse than we have heretofore seen will manifest. If godly leaders refuse to sound the alarm, deluded believers will continue to join themselves to false apostles and prophets. If leaders who love the truth do not rise up to challenge the deceivers, strong deception will form an alliance with illegitimate authority and the church will be plunged into even greater darkness.

Satan is not playing. We must identify, expose, and defeat him. We must not be dismayed when we find him hiding behind familiar faces in unexpected places. Sometimes he hides in the ranks of false apostles and prophets. Paul had to contend with "super-apostles" in 2 Corinthians 11:5. He didn't stand aside and allow them to go unchallenged. He warned the Corinthians to be on guard against their deception: "For such people are false apostles, deceitful workers, masquerading as apostles of Christ. And no wonder, for Satan himself masquerades as an angel of light. It is not surprising, then, if his servants also masquerade as servants of righteousness. Their end will be what their actions deserve" (2 Cor. 11:13–15).

There was a New Age invasion in the church in the 1970s when the materialistic prosperity gospel grew increasingly popular. I believe there was another invasion of seducing spirits that came with Eastern mysticism that joined itself to the New Age movement in the 1990s. You may have seen videos and articles circulating on the Internet that compare the manifestations of the holy laughter and Toronto Blessing movements with those which take place among Hindus in *Kundalini* awakenings.[3] I spent a couple of years early in my ministry conducting seminars to warn Christians about cults like the Children of God, Unification Church (Moonies), Christian Science, and others. I became engrossed with exposing the falsehood and deception to the point of obsession. I lost my focus for a few months but caught myself with the help of a wise older brother. He reminded me that my primary focus must always be preaching the gospel. I took his advice.

I am not on a witch hunt. I would rather be working on other books right now. I have partially completed books on missions and evangelism that are much easier for me to write. I want to put this book behind me. However, I know we are living in dangerous times and I know these things need to be addressed. I pray that I can write with sincere love for the church and the people of God. We need God's help to speak the truth in love and expose what is false without becoming negative. I realize that I may sound a bit sarcastic in writing about some of these things. I am sorry. I just think that some of them are so weird they should not be dignified with a reverent response. However, I do realize that this is a serious matter. One of my goals is to help people overcome their fear or reluctance to question and confront what they believe to be false.

It is imperative that we exercise discernment and distinguish the true from the false. It is a difficult line to walk. One thing that has helped me sort it out through the years is this observation: There is not so much hype, manipulation, and promotion around real miracles and real revivals.

There is no need for it. When real miracles happen, they speak for themselves. They don't need a manipulating soul master who knows how to work a crowd and use the media to embellish them. Excitement is spontaneous in the presence of real power; it doesn't have to be worked up when authentic miracles and healings occur.

I am not one of the skeptics who says that miracles ended with the apostles. I have seen and experienced many authentic ones. A pastor I am helping was found not breathing by his wife last month. When the paramedics arrived he was blue and his body temperature was ninety-one degrees. He entered the hospital unresponsive and full code. He was resuscitated after hours with little or no oxygen. Mistakes and complications in performing a routine tracheotomy left him in seriously critical condition in intensive care at a small hospital. He was there for several hours with 10 to 14 percent oxygen before the family and I prevailed in efforts to have him transferred to a larger hospital. Medical personnel said he wouldn't survive the transfer and encouraged the wife to leave him there and just call people she wanted to see him.

I knew what it meant to be in full code status for hours with periods of no oxygen, and then for several hours with only 14 percent oxygen. He was totally nonresponsive when I arrived at the small hospital. I didn't wait to hear doctors' reports. I went straight to intensive care—over the protests of personnel who told me I couldn't go back. I looked at the monitors, saw oxygen levels fluctuating between 10 and 14 percent, a heart that was barely beating, and lungs that were not functioning. His kidneys failed later. Upon entering the room, I quickly put my hand on his forehead, leaned down by his ear and said, "Bart, you are going to live and not die."

I spoke to his spirit and said, "Bart, your spirit is fighting. A lot of people are praying for you. Don't give up." I then remained with my hand on his forehead and prayed for hours. Doctors were honest in their assessment: they didn't expect him to make it. And if he did, the fears of the effects of brain damage from lack of oxygen were extremely unsettling. I encouraged everyone to keep believing for a miracle and said, "Bart still has a lot of work to do."

Doctors at the larger hospital did immediate emergency surgery to straighten out some of the things that had been botched. They didn't expect him to make it and also expressed grave concerns about brain damage due to oxygen deprivation. I stayed at the hospital for a couple of days and then went back and forth. Praying family and friends gathered around him. His wife left only to take showers. For six days there was no response. But on the seventh day Bart Smith came out of the coma. He pulled the tracheotomy tube out of his throat, pulled his wife down to him, and said, "I told you Jesus heals. Now get Ron Sutton. He will get me out of here." When I arrived, he was sitting up, clear minded and preaching to anyone who came in range. The anointing was so strong in the room I was nearly speechless. The doctors even had trouble talking. Bart and I are doing meetings together now. He started preaching a few days after coming out of a deep coma. By the way, should anyone be interested, we have medical verification and more pages of doctors' reports than you will even want to read. When you hear of an incredible miracle take note: It is not difficult to obtain medical records.

I believe we would see more authentic miracles if we stopped being impressed with the lying signs and wonders of the manipulators and deceivers. We will never see the real if we are content to play games with the pretenders. That is one reason I am sickened and grieved by what takes place before large crowds and on Christian television networks in America today. Miracles are marketed to make merchandise of desperate people. It is shameful. For some well-known preachers, artificial miracles bring big dividends. A short film from a mass crusade in a poor nation can net millions of dollars in support for a famous preacher. If the evangelist can get a lot of footage with the poor before he returns to the presidential suite at his high dollar hotel, it will eventually net huge returns from his viewers. The whole process has become a spectacle which has cheapened the gospel and brought reproach on the church. Many non-Christians see through the hype and understand that simple people are being exploited.

Many in the crowd know that the claims of healing are often false. The preacher asks leading questions and insecure people go along with the charade. They are overwhelmed by being brought on a platform in front of thousands of people. The lights, music, and excitement are too much for them. When the evangelist, who they view as an authority figure, begins asking questions or telling them to do something, they do and say whatever they think he wants them to.

When the footage is aired on television back home, the reports of miracles are often exaggerated even more as the evangelist sits in front of the cameras and describes the meetings to his guests and worldwide television audience. Offerings are solicited to help reach more of the poor, desperate people like the ones seen in the films; and generous support flows in. Often, only a small fraction of the money raised even goes toward international ministry. Most goes to pay for airtime, feed the evangelist's hungry ministry monster, and fund his lavish lifestyle.

We know that Jesus and His disciples were not like these modern deceivers. They didn't exploit the poor. They didn't exaggerate or embellish reports of ministry to work up a crowd. They never used miracles as a means to increase fame or raise funds. They didn't sell healings, seek seeds, or promise miracle harvests; and they didn't market prayer cloths. Jesus simply went about "doing good and healing all who were under the power of the devil because God was with him" (Acts 10:38). His unselfish love is revealed in passages like Matthew 9:35–38:

> Jesus went through all the towns and villages, teaching in their synagogues, proclaiming the good news of the kingdom and healing every disease and sickness. When he saw the crowds, he had compassion on them, because they were harassed and helpless, like sheep without a shepherd. Then he said to his disciples, "The harvest is plentiful but the workers are few. Ask the Lord of the harvest, therefore, to send out workers into his harvest field."

God is still performing miracles throughout the world, but you won't see or hear about most of them on a Christian television program. Most will take place without hype and exploitation, out of view of the cameras, in places like China, Africa, Latin America, or the slums of India where humble servants of Jesus pray in simple faith for the sick day after day. God has a great army of compassionate disciples with faith in their hearts who continually share His love with desperate people without an audience or a film crew to record their exploits. They often preach and minister under a greater anointing than the mega-ministers on television; yet, few even know their names. Most will never become famous, and it is unlikely that we will hear about them before we get to heaven. They humbly demonstrate God's power and go on their way rejoicing for the privilege of freely giving what they have freely received.

Someday we in the West will wake up and realize that the church is advancing in many parts of the world because of this army of humble disciples, not because of big television productions or famous preachers. When that realization comes, it is my prayer that God's people will place renewed emphasis on simple New Testament principles of evangelism and discipleship. God's plan for winning the world is still the church. He is still calling for laborers for the harvest fields of humanity. A great army of foot soldiers who practice personal evangelism, not a few famous television celebrities, will be the ones who get the job done and bring in the great end-time harvest.

In America we bow down at the altars of "bigness." Our deluded brains think that if it is big it must be God. But our infatuation with big names and big programs has not produced growth in the American church. We love to listen to the exaggerated claims of Christian celebrities; we love to see the crowds in big buildings and convention centers. But I fear that in our love affair with "bigness" we have lost touch with reality. The big productions have not helped the church. We have been losing ground in America for many years. Church growth has not kept pace with the growth of the population; and our ability to influence the culture has steadily diminished.

During the same period, the church in nations like China has experienced incredible growth. It has taken place without big programs, big names, or big buildings. Zealous disciples, filled with the love of Jesus, have gone into the world in places like China in simple obedience to the Great Commission. They have preached in power and have seen great miracles that were never aired on television. With little money and meager resources, they have advanced in spite of great difficulty and persecution. They have won converts one person, or sometimes one family, at a time and the church there has steadily experienced phenomenal growth. We need to learn from them.

Another great revival is coming to America. God will not allow this generation to pass without seeing a true demonstration of His power. With every great revival, there are also false manifestations. The devil is a master counterfeiter. Those of us who have experienced authentic revival, those who can distinguish between the brass and the gold, must be prepared to challenge the false. When it manifests, it must be confronted. Our generation desperately needs to remember Jude's plea:

> Beloved, while I was very diligent to write to you concerning our common salvation, I found it necessary to write to you exhorting you to contend

> earnestly for the faith which was once for all delivered to the saints
> —Jude 3, NKJV

Those who are willing to contend for the faith will find it necessary to recover something that is all but lost to this politically correct generation: the courage to confront what is false. When false prophets multiply and subtly attempt to infiltrate authentic revival, they need to be identified and exposed. The modern church is afflicted with a plague of self-proclaimed apostles and prophets who are experts at seeing a parade coming and stepping in front of it. This generation desperately needs leaders of the caliber the Apostle Paul tried to produce—leaders who preach the whole counsel of God and endeavor to handle the Scriptures with integrity. We need courageous ministers who believe that, "All Scripture is given by inspiration of God, and is profitable for doctrine, for reproof, for correction, for instruction in righteousness" (2 Tim. 3:16, NKJV).

We desperately need leaders who will follow Paul's admonition to Timothy:

> I charge you therefore before God and the Lord Jesus Christ, who will judge the living and the dead at His appearing and His kingdom: Preach the word! Be ready in season and out of season. Convince, rebuke, exhort, with all longsuffering and teaching. For the time will come when they will not endure sound doctrine, but according to their own desires, because they have itching ears, they will heap up for themselves teachers; and they will turn their ears away from the truth, and be turned aside to fables.

> But you be watchful in all things, endure afflictions, do the work of an evangelist, fulfill your ministry.
> —2 Timothy 4:1–5, nkjv

The church in America is overrun with false prophets who have learned to manipulate people with lying signs and wonders. They are making merchandise of the people of God. As the end of the age draws near, they will become more refined in their tactics and more convincing in their methods. Believers must become more grounded in the Word and hold to sound doctrine in order to resist their deception. Those who know what is going on must not become silent pretenders who act as if they don't. The time for speaking up is long past. We must learn to trust the anointing on our lives and try the spirits as the Apostle John advised: "Dear friends, do not believe every spirit, but test the spirits to see whether they are from God, because many false prophets have gone out into the world" (1 John 4:1).

We are living in the last part of the last days. The end of the age is approaching. We seem to be in the fast lane moving toward the fulfillment of Bible prophecy. The numerous warnings of Jesus and the apostles concerning deceivers in the last days should arrest our attention. Let us be diligent to guard our hearts and courageous to warn others of the insidious proliferation of deception in the church. I pray that the following passages from the apostles John and Paul will help us to move forward in faith to combat the impending outpouring of darkness and deception coming on the earth.

> Little children, it is the last hour; and as you have heard that the Antichrist is coming, even now many antichrists have come, by which we know that it is the last hour.
> —1 John 2:18, nkjv

> These things I have written to you concerning those who try to deceive you. But the anointing which you have received from Him abides in you, and you do not need that anyone teach you; but as the same anointing teaches you concerning all things, and is true, and is not a lie, and just as it has taught you, you will abide in Him.
> —1 John 2:26–27, nkjv

> Now the Spirit speaketh expressly, that in the latter times some shall depart from the faith, giving heed to seducing spirits, and doctrines of devils.
> —1 Timothy 4:1, kjv

Finally, as we deal with the deception of these last days, let us once again draw strength from God's promise given through the prophet Isaiah:

> Arise, shine; for thy light is come, and the glory of the Lord is risen upon thee. For, behold, the darkness shall cover the earth, and gross darkness the people: but the Lord shall arise upon thee, and his glory shall be seen upon thee. And the Gentiles shall come to thy light, and kings to the brightness of thy rising.
> —Isaiah 60:1–3, kjv

We need not fear. God will anoint us and use us for His glory in the midst of the darkness and the perilous times coming on the earth. Jesus is building His church and the gates of hell will not prevail against it (Matt. 16:18). Truth will trump deception and true believers will rise up in strength and victory. The brief period of peril and darkness will be followed by the return of Jesus in power and glory. We are destined to reign with Him. This is no time to retreat or give in to the oppressive darkness that is descending on the whole earth. This is the time to stir ourselves and look up in victorious faith and expectation.

> There will be signs in the sun, moon and stars. On the earth, nations will be in anguish and perplexity at the roaring and tossing of the sea. People will faint from terror, apprehensive of what is coming on the world, for the heavenly bodies will be shaken. At that time they will see the Son of Man coming in a cloud with power and great glory. When these things begin to take place, stand up and lift up your heads, because your redemption is drawing near.
> —Luke 21:25–28

Chapter 7

IT'S SUPERNATURAL, ISN'T IT?

It's supernatural, isn't it? Or is it paranormal? And if it is supernatural, is it coming from the dark or light side of supernatural? Honestly, some of it seems more super weird than supernatural. At present there is a lot of interest in the so-called supernatural and paranormal shows on secular and Christian television. Most of the interviews I have seen left me with a lot of questions. I have heard people tell stories about trips to heaven where they saw human body parts hanging around, soul travel, and swimming with a laughing blue-eyed Jesus in the river of life.

I believe in the supernatural power of God. I have since the early days of the Charismatic movement. But the stream was not so polluted then. We were experiencing a restoration of the gifts of the Spirit and discernment was among them. In those days, instead of threatening to curse us for "touching God's anointed," credible prophets and preachers challenged us to try the spirits. We questioned whether something was supernatural, fleshly, or paranormal. We questioned whether manifestations originated with God or Satan.

There was much more spontaneity and much less manipulation in our meetings back then. A wonderful supernatural outpouring was followed by a restoration of the gifts of the Spirit. Great men of God like Derek Prince taught us important truths like every revelation and prophetic utterance must be in line with the written Word; and the Word and the Spirit are always in perfect harmony and agreement.

But as time went on leaders became lax in adherence to such guidelines and more and more extrabiblical revelation entered the Charismatic movement. In some circles experience was more strongly emphasized than truth. I never had a problem with extrabiblical revelation—as long as it was biblical. With the advent of the holy laughter movement and the Toronto Blessing, less and less emphasis was placed on the written Word and extrabiblical prophecies and experiences went way off the tracks. While we laughed, the numbers of self-appointed (or quickly and wrongly appointed) apostles and prophets grew and the charismatic church moved farther and farther away from the Bible. Balanced teachers were replaced with unbalanced prophets who refused to be encumbered with sound doctrine or the rules of hermeneutics. They began saying whatever came into their spirits, or their minds, at conferences and meetings everywhere. Large conference centers across the nation filled up with people hoping to receive a personal word from a "prophet" they didn't know.

It got a little strange at conferences. After a time of worship, prophetic words, and a smorgasbord of extrabiblical revelations, people went forward for personal ministry. An army of "prophets" and "prayer warriors" came out of the crowd and it was on. Some people went down immediately upon being touched and having someone say "fire" or "fill." Others stayed on their feet and they tended to have a better chance of getting a personal word. A lot of "prophets" just walked back and forth and repeatedly said, "More, more." It was sometimes interesting simply watching it all. Many of the new prophets had received their credentials after sending checks to "paper mills." The chief dispenser of prophet licenses is now a highly esteemed leader—Bishop, Prophet, Dr., Apostle—in the New Apostolic Reformation. (Those were his titles in order of succession.) Many of his fellow prophets and apostles also have the contagious disease of "Titlemania." One of them became a Presiding Apostle and later an Ambassadorial Apostle. He did earn the letters behind his name, but you won't find the titles he wore in the Bible. I never did understand why preachers send money to "paper mills" to get pieces of paper with titles and letters they never earned. No one is ever going to ask questions about your credentials anyway. You can appoint and call yourself whatever you want to in charismatic circles these days.

When it became popular to be a prophet, preachers sent money to "paper mills" to get a certificate with "Prophet" in front of their names. They printed new cards and handed them out everywhere. I wondered for awhile, if the trend continued, whether we would have anything but prophets in the church. But that was before leaders of the New Apostolic Reformation decided that apostles had more authority than prophets. I violated protocol a few times and asked about the ordaining institution of a few apostles, bishops, doctors, and prophets. I should write a book on the responses. I learned that a number of guys got them down south after attending a prophets' school for two or three days, where they practiced prophecy in groups before being commissioned by the exalted leader.

Experts on prophecy and spiritual warfare came like restless termites out of the woodwork and found homes in the prayer movement, the Toronto Blessing, and the International House of Prayer and its affiliates. New revelations came forth everywhere, and people suddenly seemed to be more excited about going to a meeting to get a personal word than they were about hearing a message from the written Word. The focus shifted from body ministry, with individual members moving in the gifts, to leaders doing it all from up front. We became spectators waiting for a word from the "anointed" prophets who circulated among us.

We made some of them superstars and acted as though they were infallible. When being a prophet was no longer as popular as being an apostle, the "paper mills" were ecstatic. Some took grand titles to themselves and began acting like the "super apostles" Paul was so disgusted with in 2 Corinthians 11:5. Others started calling themselves generals—and we let them get away with it.

Believers who didn't like to read the Bible gobbled up prophetic words like little children who were given pieces of candy. We ignored Paul's commendation of the Bereans and didn't seriously check the accuracy of the words given by the great prophets. Some of us are crying for believers to remember it now: "Now the Berean Jews were of more noble character than those in Thessalonica, for they received the message with great eagerness and examined the scriptures every day to see if what Paul said was true" (Acts 17:11). Wow! We should take a lesson from those guys. They even scrutinized and checked what the great Apostle Paul said to see if it lined up with the written Word.

Our problem was twofold: We stopped functioning as the body of Christ and became spectators; and we got lazy and gave apostles and prophets too much leeway. We even made excuses for the ones who messed up and started viewing their performance the way managers of baseball teams look at batting averages. One famous false prophet, who liked to have young women disrobe before him so they could stand naked before the Lord, defended all his strikeouts by saying that New Testament prophets weren't judged by the same standard as their Old Testament predecessors. He estimated that prophets today had a 15 to 35 percent rate of accuracy. I think he was on the low side of 15 percent. That made him a minor leaguer but you wouldn't have known it by the way big league managers of ministries and television networks treated him. I nailed him before he was famous but my Vineyard pastor friends didn't believe me. They were enamored with the old faker.

We accepted more and more extrabiblical revelations without really questioning them or doing what the Bereans did. The "extra" in extrabiblical kept going farther and farther away from the written Word. We let go of safeguards that had protected us and the train left the rails. More and more unscriptural, extrabiblical, and "selectively" biblical revelation contaminated the waters.

The stream is extremely polluted today; some

disillusioned charismatics have grown so tired of the contamination that they have become suspicious of all things supernatural. I can't blame them but I am concerned about what many are doing in reaction. Charismatic and Pentecostal churches throughout the nation have embraced the seeker-sensitive philosophy of ministry and no longer allow the gifts of the Spirit to operate in their services. Many charismatic and Pentecostal believers grew so tired of swimming in contaminated waters, they didn't even want to stay in the Spirit-filled churches that were dialing down. When scandals involving high profile leaders became public, they ran for cover to seeker-friendly and mainline churches where the gifts of the Spirit were never manifest. It felt safer. At least the leaders didn't seem to be polluting the waters with so much greed, falsehood, and immorality.

Charismatic Christians who placed a high premium on integrity in the ministry became disillusioned. Their decision to get out of the water was understandable—but it was also dangerous. The enemies of the gospel will never be defeated without genuine Pentecostal power. We must not sacrifice the true power of God out of revulsion over what the deceivers have done. I am as sick of charlatans and proud, titled pretenders as anyone else; but I am not going to let go of what I know to be real because of the fakers. We desperately need a fresh infusion of the authentic power of God now more than ever. We need a restoration of all the gifts of the Spirit (See my book *Sacred Fire: Why Don't We Try Pentecost One More Time*, also published by Creation House, for more on the need for the power of the Holy Spirit.) We need to get the emphasis off of the superstars who are happy to let us be spectators; some of them just want us to watch their shows and keep the offerings coming. We need to become active participants once again and find leaders who truly want the Holy Spirit to direct and govern our meetings.

We must not reject the real in order to guard against the false. Moving from troubled charismatic waters that have been contaminated by immoral leaders to the calm waters of seeker-sensitive religion is not the answer. There might not seem to be as much danger in the calmer waters, but it is an illusion. It is dangerous to become a spectator who just sits back and relaxes to enjoy an entertaining service and listen to a nonthreatening message. You can become spiritually lazy and grow sleepy in calm waters. And this is no time to fall asleep—spiritual danger is all around us.

We need to be awake and alert. We need to be filled with the supernatural power of God in order to combat the forces of darkness. Our spiritual enemies operate with supernatural power and attack us with supernatural weapons. It is ludicrous to think that we can resist, much less overcome, them without the supernatural power of God. That is one reason I don't understand why leaders in the seeker-sensitive movement run from the power of the Holy Spirit. Most absolutely refuse to allow the gifts of the Spirit to operate in their services. They are running from the supernatural as the world seems to be running to it. And I really don't understand how any Pentecostal or charismatic leader who was baptized with the real Holy Spirit could even entertain thoughts of running for cover in seeker-friendly religion. To me, that is paramount to denying the Holy Spirit. At best, it is to seriously grieve Him.

However, I do sympathize with believers who are fed up with the crazy manifestations and never ending extra-biblical revelations in spurious movements of recent years. Couple the crazy manifestations with the immoral lives of some of the leaders, and it is not difficult to understand why so many sincere believers are disgusted. But we must not allow our frustration to produce a wrong reaction. Running from the supernatural is not the right response. The Apostle Paul certainly didn't think it was. When he encountered confusion in the church at Corinth, he didn't run from the supernatural or try to shut it down. He simply endeavored to address the confusion, bring correction, and inject order into the mess. And it was probably a bigger mess than we have today; he had to contend with the influence of the pantheon of Greek and Roman gods and their mystery religions.

I, like many of you, am disturbed that so much reproach has come on the church because of impostors who traffic in the false and get away with selling it as real; but I am not going to run from the wonder and glory of the authentic because of the false among us. We need to learn from Paul and the apostles of the New Testament. They didn't run for cover or restrict the gifts of the Spirit because false prophets were on the loose. They confronted the false prophets, corrected false teachings, and continued to move in the Spirit. Leaders in the early church practiced confrontation; their writings are shot through with challenges to false teachers and warnings to believers in danger of being deceived by them. But they never once suggested that the gifts of the Spirit should be shut down because of the confusion that sometimes came with deception or a lack of wisdom and maturity among believers.

Paul began 1 Corinthians 14 with these words, "Follow the way of love and eagerly desire gifts of the Spirit, especially prophecy." After devoting the rest of the chapter to instruction and correction, he concluded by saying, "Therefore, my brothers and sisters, be eager to prophesy, and do not forbid speaking in tongues. But everything should be done in a fitting and orderly way" (1 Cor. 14:39–40). I don't understand how any leader could read those words and then deny or take action to shut down all supernatural manifestations of the Holy Spirit. Every authentic leader who loves the body of Christ is concerned about the damage false movements and manifestations have done. But leaders who know that authentic supernatural power has existed throughout eternity surely should not attempt to restrict it this late in the game. We need the real to combat the false—inside and outside the church. To forbid the manifestation of the authentic leaves us defenseless against the false. To fail to confront the false with truth and authentic spiritual authority gives the advantage to the deceivers.

Reasonable leaders know that we must recover the lost art of confrontation. We cannot continue to let the false go unchallenged. But given the ever increasing interest in the New Age movement, paranormal activity, Eastern religions, Satanism, and various forms of witchcraft in modern society, it certainly doesn't make sense to run from the supernatural in the church. There will always be a mixture. That is why there is such a desperate need for leaders who rightly divide the Word of truth (2 Tim. 2:15, NKJV) and who are able to discern between both good and evil (Heb. 5:14, NKJV). Understanding the dilemma put me in a quandary. I got it: I understood why some leaders were so concerned over false manifestations that they decided to buy into a movement that advocated restricting the supernatural; but I still don't understand how they can read the Bible and justify their position.

In guarding against false or fleshly manifestations, leaders of the seeker-sensitive movement decided to completely ignore what the Holy Spirit said through Paul. They took action to totally forbid the operation of the gifts of the Spirit in their services. A megachurch that was known nationwide for anointed worship and the moving of the Spirit did it. I am still in shock fifteen years later. The pastor grew so tired of the foolishness that came with the holy laughter movement, he just shut it all down. His biggest concern was the effect of so-called supernatural manifestations on lost people. Now he doesn't even call them lost anymore. When he waved the white flag and ran from the foolishness, they were transformed from lost sinners into unchurched seekers. Another church I started did the same thing after a brief dance with holy laughter.

I am fed up with the foolishness too; but I can't scripturally support the position of those who forbid the operation of the gifts. My stand has cost me, but I can't agree with what these leaders have done; it seems like a clear violation of what Paul so clearly shared with the Corinthians. The KJV says succinctly in 1 Corinthians 14:39: "forbid not to speak with tongues." Leaders of the seeker-sensitive movement are aware of the growing interest in the supernatural among the unchurched seekers they target with their philosophy of ministry. So, why do they deem it wise to restrict the gifts of the Spirit altogether? I have concluded that the manifestations of the foolish and the false, coupled with ideas stemming from our scientific Western mindset, must have been too much for them. They did the unthinkable—they threw the baby out with the bath water. Out of fear of the false and the confusion it brings, they restricted and in some cases totally rejected the real.

It didn't concern me greatly until charismatic and Pentecostal leaders I knew began to embrace the seeker-sensitive philosophy of ministry. I knew there had to be more to it than simple overreaction to weirdness. That is when I began to think a little more deeply about Paul's warnings concerning seducing spirits in the last days. I knew that only strong delusion could enable this philosophy of ministry to gain so much traction and make inroads into charismatic and Pentecostal churches.

It is a bit audacious for a puny human being to take it upon himself to tell the all powerful Holy Spirit when and how He may move: Wouldn't you agree? What are we thinking? Is the Holy Spirit supposed to ask the permission of mortals before moving in our midst? However, I now hasten to say that we all know that much of what is called supernatural today *is not*. We have to stop pretending not to know. It is time for us to stand up like men and confront the foolishness like Paul did.

I now want to reason with those who still highly esteem authentic expressions of the supernatural power of God—those who would never dare to forbid them. It is imperative that credible leaders address the problems that have resulted from foolishness, fakery, and deception. We have tolerated manipulation, weirdness, and lack of order to our own detriment and to that of the church. The world is watching and laughing. Some on the outside, who are actually rooting for us, are holding their breath and standing on tiptoe waiting for leaders to address some of the excess and nonsensical behavior. They would like to see a few credible leaders address the confusion and lack of order as Paul did in Corinth. Maybe this would be a good time for the leaders of the laughing revivals, who seem to now be trying to distance themselves from past indiscretions, to make public statements. Lost people, who look in from outside, must be wondering if the modern church is overrun with preachers who are afraid to confront anything.

We don't get a pass. We are compelled to do what earlier generations have done: confront what we know to be false. Often, what we allow to operate under the supernatural banner today is nothing more than superficial emotionalism. There is no power in it, and we know it. What we allow to be called supernatural would often be better classified as super weird, super exaggerated, super imagined, super embellished, or super made up. Surely we can find the strength to expose and confront falsehood and deception, and also the intelligence to do it without rejecting the real.

To me, it makes no sense to reject the genuine because the counterfeit exists. We don't stop spending money, or restrict its use, because counterfeit bills are circulating in the money stream along with the authentic. We simply try to sort out the real from the false. Shouldn't we do the same thing in the spiritual realm: endeavor to keep the genuine flowing while simultaneously trying to identify and remove the false from the stream? I take testimonies of supernatural experiences with a grain of salt—a lot of them sound more paranormal or imagined than supernatural these days. But I am not going to forget that I serve a supernatural God who is still working powerfully today.

So, what can we do? First, we must remember that the world is watching. I mean it when I say that some people are actually curious to see what we will do. They need to see us demonstrate greater integrity: integrity that compels us to stop making excuses for the weirdness we have allowed to operate under the banner of the supernatural. While I have been amazed at Christians who were quick to totally reject the supernatural, I have also been a bit incredulous to see how easy it has been to deceive those who are obsessed with the supernatural. A preacher who knows how to work a crowd can provoke fleshly displays of emotionalism and call it the moving of the Spirit, and without thinking half the crowd will immediately jump in the water with him. And the world is watching.

After a meeting, excited believers can't wait to rush out and tell the watching world that all the weirdness was really the supernatural power of God in operation. Skeptics look for the exaggerated hype on Facebook. It always appears during and after a meeting saturated with weirdness. And silly seekers of the sensational never disappoint the skeptics and their friends. Even the courtesy drops given to powerless purveyors of false doctrine and spurious manifestations are tagged as a supernatural. The carpet lovers don't admit that they just dropped courteously—after making certain a catcher was behind them; they proclaim that they were slain in the Spirit. Will somebody please join me in saying loudly, "Pretending and allowing what we know to be false always cheapens what is real in the eyes of a watching world." I don't understand why so few of God's people, especially leaders who know better, don't challenge or expose the foolishness. Why do we pretend and play along with it? If we ever want to see more real miracles, we will be required to demonstrate a much higher degree of integrity. Do we really need someone to explain to us why the world and the evangelical church are laughing at us?

I am a firm believer in the supernatural. I pray daily for a greater release of the power and gifts of the Holy Spirit. I am not on lockdown at the mercy of my intellect or a scientific Western mindset. I see no contradiction between science and the supernatural. Countless healings took place in our crusades among the poor and the desperate in Africa, Asia, and Latin America. They were desperate because doctors and medicine were not available, even if they would have had money to pay for them. It was either Jesus or a visit to a witchdoctor. Amazing healings took place in that atmosphere of desperation. I believe in the supernatural. I just don't believe that a lot of what is labeled supernatural in America today is authentic. Sometimes what is called a supernatural manifestation is nothing more than flesh and emotion unhinged, or weird or paranormal behavior.

The modern church has been infatuated with so called supernatural movements that were characterized by a lot of foolish unruly behavior. Thinker alert: The supernatural moving of the Holy Spirit can be strange but it is never weird. Most people think *strange* and *weird* mean basically the same thing. They don't; and it is interesting to study the difference. The modern meaning associated with *weird* is much different than that of its old English origins. Older dictionaries often use synonyms like "eerie, bizarre, or uncanny" to describe it.[1] In earlier times it was often associated with witchcraft. *Noah Webster's 1828 Dictionary* lists it as an adjective with the meaning "skilled in witchcraft."[2] I came across several instances in old dictionaries where weird was associated with witchcraft.

> The use of weird as a synonym for witch was quite common in Scotland [as we can see from] Peter Heylin's Microcosmus of 1625: "These two...were mette by three Fairies, or Witches (Weirds the Scots call them)."...The phrase *weird sister* is found in several manuscripts leading up to its most famous appearance in Shakespeare's *Macbeth*.[3]

I consulted numerous old dictionaries on my shelves and found almost no references to *strange* associated with witchcraft. It is associated more with definitions of supernatural. Weird is more often associated with witchcraft. You may think I am "straining at gnats" here, but I think the distinction is worth noting. *Dictionary.com* says that "*strange* implies that the thing or its cause is unknown or unexplained."[4] *Merriam-Webster Online* also includes these meanings: "exciting wonder or awe: extraordinary."[5] *Collins* adds: "Not easily explained: *a strange phenomenon*."[6] We might be wise to exercise ourselves in the hard work of thinking the next time we hear of a revival or new movement characterized by bizarre supernatural manifestations: Are they strange or weird?

Supernatural has two sides: darkness and light, Satan and God. We should endeavor to discern the source of manifestations; and it would not hurt to ask ourselves if they are weird or strange. We should also keep in mind that some manifestations are not supernatural at all. Sometimes they are nothing more than fleshly displays of emotion that occur when some people get excited and sometimes when encouraged by a manipulative, false prophet. The only supernatural manifestations you are likely to see in these instances will be the work of demons that like to hang out with dishonest leaders; some of them will do almost anything to stir up a crowd. In such cases, what appears to be spectacular may actually be nothing more than a spectacle.

Let's admit it: American charismatics are gullible. Our Western mindsets have influenced us to lean toward science for answers but we remain infatuated with the supernatural. We are careless with it because we don't respect it as we should. The supernatural can be found in two realms: darkness and light. The light is for the pure in heart who know God. Playing games with the supernatural, failing to walk in obedience to God, and neglecting the disciplines of prayer and Bible study can leave Christians vulnerable to influence from the dark side. I am convinced that the Charismatic movement was contaminated when believers left the rails of orthodox Christianity in the 1970s to pursue a materialistic prosperity message. And I think it happened again in the 1990s when we began pursuing exhilarating experiences and welcoming manifestations that had no basis in the Bible. Leaders manipulated crowds with influences they allowed to control them and called the manifestations that were produced the moving of the Holy Spirit. That is dangerous ground to walk on. Calling flesh and emotion the work of the Spirit opens the door for seducing spirits.

People in India live in fear of supernatural forces that torment them. They desperately seek ways to appease them and find relief. They worship inanimate objects and just about anything that swims, walks, or crawls. The pervasiveness and cruelty of Hinduism has held almost an entire culture in bondage and oppression for centuries. Yet, in our ignorance and naiveté, we have opened ourselves up to influences common in Hindu rituals. Most of the bizarre manifestations of the holy laughter and Toronto Blessing movements are also common in Hinduism—as are the sinking spells and severe depression that tormented many people after they got drunk in the spirit and were hit with the holy laughter anointing.

We are too gullible. Americans flock to watch movies filled with witchcraft and Hinduism and don't even realize what they are watching. The popular movies about avatars are straight out of ancient Hinduism. You can read about them in Sanskrit writings, and the works of Hindu masters. Their blue color should have been a clue for anyone who is aware of the Hindu deity Vishnu and his incarnations like Krishna.[7] Avatars are messengers of the gods in Hinduism. They are manifestations of a Hindu deity in a physical form: "the human or animal form of a Hindu god on earth."[8] We really should become informed about the *Kundalini* spirit of Hinduism[9] and take note that Hindus were experiencing manifestations common in the holy laughter and Toronto Blessing movements.

I have talked with many Christians who saw the *Avatar* movies. I have yet to speak with one who knew what they were watching. I am not saying you should never watch a movie like that. I am saying we should be a little better informed. Just so the *Avatar* fans won't think I am pulling this out of the air, allow me to quote a Hindu writer of the early twentieth century:

> When the *Kundalini* again wants to raise up from ignorance to Mighty Wisdom, and a Blissful state, she chooses India again, for the purpose of raising India once more to the highest of Pure Wisdom. In ages past the greatest *Avatars* (author's emphasis) of India—...Ram Sri, Sri Krishna...Buddha and countless others...[10]

It is no wonder that false prophets with a knack for manipulation can so easily prey on charismatic Christians. We are desirous of the supernatural but we are not diligent to exercise our spiritual senses to determine whether manifestations emanate from light, darkness, or the flesh. Before we dive headlong into the next movement that comes down the path, we might do well to remember that Satan has the ability to transform himself into an angel of light; some of his most deceptive apostles are pretenders who masquerade as ministers of righteousness (2 Cor. 11:14–15). Given the darkness and deception of the days we find ourselves living in, let me say without reservation: We don't need another extrabiblical prophet or apostle—we need more godly pastors who will guard their flocks and be watchmen on the wall.

Before I look for an exit ramp for this chapter, I want to revisit the question: Is it supernatural or paranormal? While a supernatural event or manifestation can in some senses be considered paranormal, there is normally a big difference in meaning. We should be more careful with what we label supernatural. Paranormal and supernatural are seldom synonymous. *Paranormal* is an adjective most people associate with ghosts or haunted houses and places. It is actually used to describe a wide range of phenomena which are outside the range of normal experience or scientific explanation.[11] It is also often associated with aliens and UFO's and in conjunction with psychic and occult activities such as clairvoyance, extrasensory perception, and telepathy.

The popular 1984 Columbia Pictures movie *Ghostbusters* both revealed and fueled a worldwide interest in paranormal activity. It set a record for Columbia Pictures at the time of its release grossing $23 million its first week.[12] Its success resulted in sequels; and numerous movies and television shows about paranormal activity were inspired by it. Since its release, the proliferation of paranormal groups worldwide has been astounding. I have talked with members of such groups who are involved in exorcisms of haunted houses and demon-possessed people. Many have no idea what they are actually dealing with and seldom realize the dangers. There is nothing funny about real "ghost busting" activity.

Before offering more information on paranormal activity, I want to comment a bit more on the supernatural.

Supernatural beings are spiritual and are found in both the kingdom of God and the kingdom of darkness. In recent times, things like werewolves and vampires are often referred to as supernatural beings. But the term *supernatural* is most often used in reference to God and His angels or Satan and demons. The Christian's fight is "against principalities, against powers, against the rulers of the darkness of this age, against spiritual hosts of wickedness in the heavenly places" (Eph. 6:12, NKJV). We are engaged in a life and death struggle with supernatural spiritual beings from the dark side. Thankfully, we have some heavenly allies in the fight—angels who didn't join Lucifer in his rebellion (Heb. 1:14).

I recently dealt with a "pastor" who was a member of the paranormal society in his county. After a few questions, I learned of his obsession with paranormal events and his activities with the local paranormal society which was comprised of mostly non-Christians. *It's Supernatural* was his favorite television show and *Ghostbusters* was his favorite movie. When he called himself an exorcist and described the group's experiences of cleansing haunted houses and driving demons out of people, I was appalled that he could also call himself a pastor. I didn't believe the methods employed by the group could actually drive a ghost out of a house or a demon out of a person, but I asked him a few questions anyway. The first was, "Why would a Christian pastor collaborate with agnostics and unbelievers to cast out demons?" The second was, "Have you considered that demons you drive out might be finding a new home in some of the members of your group who are not protected by the blood of Jesus?"

His response revealed that he was the airhead of airheads. He said, "Oh, no. That is not possible. We command them to go to the dry places and never return." He was so confused I felt pity for him. I told him that he didn't have a license to lock demons up in the dry places, but demons had a license to operate here as long as there were people who allowed it. I discussed several scriptures with him and suggested that he reconsider his involvement with such a group. He was adamant about continuing his ministry as a pastor and maintaining his membership in the paranormal society. He became visibly upset and left abruptly when I explained that a merger of the two churches was out of the question.

I next encountered him about a month later at a meeting of about thirty pastors and leaders from the area. He had them onboard to help support a meeting. He wanted to bring in a speaker who had appeared on his favorite show: *It's Supernatural*. I knew about the speaker he was planning to bring into the area and had some real concerns about him. The great preacher who was coming to town had one claim to fame: an appearance on the aforementioned show where he had, several years before, been given the opportunity to tell his bizarre story. His video of the show on which he was interviewed gave him credibility with Christians who didn't take the time to do a little research.

The paranormal pastor had the leaders excited about bringing him to town. He invited everyone to attend a planning meeting the following week and announced that a representative from the ministry would be there to give more information and answer questions. I was flabbergasted at the gullibility of those pastors and leaders. I didn't need more information but I did show up the following week with a few questions.

The representative came as promised the next week, but he was not expecting questions. He wasn't accustomed to getting any. Leaders in city after city normally just let him and his paranormal friend slip into town without any serious questioning—and then slip out with a lot of money. He became visibly upset when I raised questions. His eyes had sparkled earlier as he filled the room with hype about the great leader he wanted to bring to town. He made it sound as if the guy was just a notch under the Godhead. He stuttered as he cautioned me about the danger of touching "God's anointed." Amazingly, I was the only person in the group of some thirty charismatic pastors and leaders who had any questions to ask. He mistakenly assumed that because I was so outnumbered he could just disregard my irritating questions. I remained silent after his threat and let him move on.

The front man went on to describe how the great leader he was representing had died and gone to heaven. He explained that he had been skeptical himself until he read the medical records that confirmed the death and miraculous return to the land of the living. At that point I interrupted to insert another question: "Would you be willing to provide those records for our review?" Negative: He quickly explained that it was the policy of the ministry not to provide them. They didn't want to come into an area if pastors were skeptical. Most of the excited leaders were not at all disturbed by his lack of disclosure. However, several were upset that I was asking questions! The representative thought the wind was blowing his way and tried to blow past me to other topics of discussion.

He actually tried to intimidate me by cautioning me again to be careful of judging and touching "God's anointed." He even related a couple of incidents of tragedy that had befallen people who had done so in the past. After years of war on many fields of battle, I have become rather bored with those kinds of underhanded attempts at intimidation. Undaunted, I went on to explain that I liked to know a bit about a speaker before I lent credibility to an event by putting my name on it, or giving support to it, and then moved on to my next question.

I posed it to the group of leaders: "Have any of you who have agreed to promote this meeting read the proposed speaker's book which describes his experience?"[13] None had, so I said, "I did read it, and I happen to have a copy with me. Is anyone interested in hearing at least some of what the speaker you are being asked to endorse saw and experienced on his journey to heaven?"

The reaction was: I came under attack! A pastor asked rather angrily, "Who do you think you are to question an anointed man of God like this?" I responded, "You said earlier that you didn't know him or his representative. How do you know he is anointed; and, more importantly, what do you know about his life and character?"

His response helped me understand why so many con men can get away with making merchandise of the people of God. He simply said, "I saw him on a video. He's anointed."

My response to that naïve remark was, "The devil is anointed, but I wouldn't want to endorse one of his meetings." All hell broke loose. A woman across the room jerked her head toward me in a manner which I think has to be humanly impossible and, with eyes bulging, yelled in a deep throated, masculine sounding voice, "I know you." I looked at her and said calmly, "I know you too. I have dealt with you all over the world." I heard a pastor behind me ask a young leader, "Where does he know her from?" The young leader responded, "I don't think he was addressing the woman." That young leader was the only one who seemed to understand what was going on in the room. I felt worse than Daniel in the lions' den—my lions didn't have lockjaw.

The representative interrupted the silence that followed the confrontation by saying, "I think we have had just about enough of his questions. Let's move on." But finally an elderly sister found her voice and said, "I don't know about the rest of you, but I am interested in hearing some of what Ron discovered in that book." When a few others expressed the same sentiment, I began to share some of the most bizarre accounts.

I told how the author had been met at heaven's gate by a friend who had beaten him there. After the friend took him to his mansion, the journey continued to a room filled with unformed blobs of flesh. His friend's description of what they were is too disturbing to even repeat here. He was then led into a room filled with spare body parts of every description. Angels carried them to earth when someone needed a creative miracle. After referencing the pages which related this weird experience, my question for the group of leaders was: "Does anyone think that blobs of flesh can get into heaven? Do you honestly believe that

God needs to keep spare body parts hanging around?" With those questions, I seemed to gain a few more friends, and a respected elder asked me to continue. The representative then excused himself and the poor paranormal pastor was left standing all alone before the now animated group of leaders.

An evangelist next to me, who had been thumbing through the book I took to the meeting, asked me to comment on an alleged account of the man swimming in the river of life. I shared how he described meeting Jesus and looking into the most beautiful blue eyes he had ever seen. The evangelist said that the last time he checked Jesus' eyes had become flames of fire. I responded that I had met many pure-blooded Jews but I had yet to meet one with blue eyes. It was beginning to dawn on the group of overly trusting leaders that they had been dangerously close to lending credibility to a man who was way off the tracks.

After peering into those deep blue eyes, Jesus allegedly took him to the river and they swam, splashed, laughed, and played around together. He then told how he could feel debris from earth being washed off in the crystal clear water. I then asked the group, "Does anyone here honestly believe that debris from earth can enter heaven?"

A few simple questions were all it took to sabotage the plot. Nearly all of the leaders decided not to lend credibility to such nonsense by endorsing the meeting. Shouldn't we all be asking more questions? It is no wonder the world is laughing at us. You don't even have to know the Bible to realize that bizarre accounts like this are often filled with fabrications from a vivid imagination—or from a rattled brain, or from a seducing spirit, or from a creative con man who is cashing in on a naïve obsession with the supernatural.

I believe strongly in supernatural experiences and encounters, but I don't check my brain at the door when I go into a meeting to listen to someone's testimony. I think we can agree that it is time for credible leaders in charismatic and Pentecostal churches to put on badges and start policing this mess. If we don't, people like the "Bible Answer Man" and his deputies will get the badges by default.

Chapter 8

HOLY LAUGHTER, BATMAN!

Relax. The title is just geared to get your attention. If you are an enamored fan of holy laughter, don't put this book down. Trust me: I take the phenomenon of holy laughter, and all the bizarre manifestations that came with it, very seriously. I know that it is not just a laughing matter. Multitudes say they were blessed by it; but it also caused strife and division and wrecked churches around the world. When holy laughter broke out in the early 1990s, we were desperate for a fresh move of God. For awhile it looked like we had found a shortcut to revival.

But the movement quickly subsided and most don't refer to it as a revival. The hoped for harvest of lost souls never came in. The holy laughter movement and the Toronto Blessing were tragic mixtures of truth and error, flesh and Spirit. From the beginning respected leaders raised concerns about extrabiblical and unbiblical practices and behaviors; but they were ignored. A departure from the written Word caused the movements to go too far into uncharted, extrabiblical territory. Experience was exalted over the Bible, which left the door open to deception. Seducing spirits and doctrines of demons quickly moved through the door and brought all manner of weirdness into our midst. The charismatic church has never been more confused—and never so far from the Bible.

So, why do I want to talk about this so long after the heyday of holy laughter? Because I believe it opened the door for an invasion by false prophets and deceiving spirits. Even greater dangers lie ahead; but experience-oriented, sign-seeking believers don't see it. They are deficient in discernment. Many recklessly chase after every new phenomenon and don't even detect the darkness closing in around them. They have launched out into the turbulent sea of extrabiblical revelation without the Bible for a compass. A storm is looming on the horizon, and it has not even registered on their spiritual radar screens. Their deception detectors aren't even in the on position. False prophets are at every bend in the road, yet many cruise along never hearing a warning signal. Here's what my spiritual radar detector is doing: Beep! Beep, beep! Beep, beep, beep!!!

Jesus' warnings about false prophets and Paul's warnings about seducing spirits and doctrines of demons are unknown or ignored by many charismatic believers today. In forty years of worldwide ministry, I have never seen God's people more careless or riper for deception. They follow false prophets off the road chasing the newest supernatural or paranormal manifestation without regard for the dangers. Spiritual highs and ecstatic experiences have become more important than anointed preaching. The reason experience-oriented believers are often oblivious to spiritual danger is because they are not grounded in the Word of God. Many in this generation would rather get a personal word from a man they don't know than a word from God by reading their own Bibles. False prophets love it.

How much foolishness will we have to see before we recognize what is among us and begin to call it by its first name—*False*? Do we need a man to wear a sign that says "I am a false prophet" before we will be able to perceive what he is? How weird or bizarre does it have to become before we start asking questions? For those who have had their fill of deception and unfulfilled prophecies, I will give a few characteristics of false prophets. First, they all like money—and they will use crazy gimmicks and all manner of manipulation to get it. Mark it down: It's all about the money. False prophets just want you to be a generous spectator who watches their shows. Forget about body ministry; they want to run the whole show. The only time they want your participation is during the offering. They want you to be dependent on them. Drink the wine of false prophets long enough and you will become like a drunk who keeps going back to the bar, or a junkie who makes regular visits to a drug dealer. It is costly to enter into a codependent relationship with manipulative deceivers.

Secondly, false prophets like lots of extrabiblical revelation. They don't want to be encumbered or restrained by the written Word. In fact, most modern ones almost always exalt experience over truth. They are weak in the Word—but always ready to give you a personal word. And they won't encourage you to diligently study the Bible because if you do that, you will soon recognize them for what they are. The messages and manifestations of false prophets won't stand up under a theological test. They know it and that is why they won't even attempt to defend their extrabiblical, or unbiblical, experiences and bizarre manifestations with Scripture. And, again, that is why you won't hear them exhorting you to diligently study the Bible. If charismatic believers become biblically literate, it will put them out of business. Christians who are grounded in the Word are not impressed by false prophets nor moved by the manifestations they manufacture.

Thirdly, false prophets often do bizarre things to attract attention and gain publicity. Once they get noticed, they utilize continual hype to stay in the limelight. It is common for false prophets to make many claims of miracles that can never be verified. They are masters at getting insecure people to play along with them and testify about a miracle they never received. Such people almost always try to do what they think the authority figure wants them to do. Delusion is so strong today that false prophets can often work their game even after they have been exposed. Some enamored followers of false prophets are in such spiritual fog, they wouldn't recognize truth if it slapped them in the face.

Do you remember what Jesus said: "Blessed are they that hunger and thirst for *manifestations* for they shall be filled"? Well, that's not exactly what He said, is it? (See Matthew 5:6.) But given the way some charismatics act, you would *think* it was what He said. Many people are seeking manifestations of God more than they are seeking God. In fact, some are almost worshipping manifestations.

That always happens when Christians make a god out of experience. That's dangerous: When truth is sacrificed in pursuit of an experience, the door is opened to seducing spirits. It is my observation that believers who develop a dependence on feelings and ecstatic experiences tend to neglect the written Word. That's what the false prophets want you to do. A person who is well acquainted with the authentic is not easily deceived by the counterfeit.

During times of true revival there is always hunger for truth. Believers pick up their Bibles and read to satisfy that hunger. They are open to prophetic words but they are not driven by a need to seek them. They are more enthralled with a Bible full of words from God than personal words from men.

In authentic revivals people are always excited about the Bible. It comes alive to them. They fall in love with it all over again. They don't go to meetings just to see something or receive an impartation; they go to hear the Word of God preached in power. It's not that way right now. Today, if my primary goals were to fill up buildings and receive big offerings, I would do just what the false prophets are doing. I would never think of trying to do it with powerful, Bible-based preaching. That is the old-fashioned way to make a movement. Today you just find out where people itch and scratch it. You have to entertain them, or stir up their emotions, or give them something a bit weird. If I wanted to fill a building I would just start jerking and twitching and making weird noises when I got in the pulpit. I would stagger around like a drunkard and speak with a slur or an imitated accent. I would tell a few jokes and laugh at them myself. I would then say something like, "The anointing is all over me. Come up here and get some of this."

There are always a few in any crowd who will respond to that invitation. I would then concentrate on getting the most desperate and insecure among the respondents worked up. A man who understands group dynamics can manipulate a few people and induce herd behavior in most of the rest. Soon he will have a crowd and weirdness will manifest all around him. Weird behavior and laughter are contagious. The giggling gurus of Hinduism figured that out long before holy laughter hit America.

No sir! If I wanted to gather a crowd these days, I wouldn't try to do it with powerful preaching of the truth. In fact, I would subjugate truth to experience and put the emphasis on emotional release and ecstatic feelings. I would act a little weird and entice a few others to jump in the river with me. I would get the crowd worked up and send them home on a high note. And just before I let my armor bearers open the doors, I would tell them to invite their friends and post on social media. I would tell them, "We are going to see even greater things tomorrow." Then I would call the local papers, television, and radio stations and exaggerate what took place and tell them they better get somebody there to cover it. They are almost always anxious to cover another meeting that makes "tongue talkers" look weird. If a man has a little personality power, plays his cards right, and gets a little help from seducing spirits, he can make a movement out of that. Ask me how I know it will work? It has already been done—many times.

I know. Someone is going to argue that the word of faith guys started a movement by preaching the "word." That's what the seducing spirits want you to believe. The truth is; there is not much Word preached by "word" preachers. The small portion they do preach is very carefully selected. Where have you been? Word of faith preachers didn't make their movement by preaching the Word. They just diagnosed a materialistic itch for blessing and prosperity and scratched it. But enough about them; that is a future book entitled *Of Money and Men*.

Many charismatics thought their search for a fresh experience was over when holy laughter broke out at Carpenter's Home Church in Lakeland, Florida, in 1993. Testimonies of people getting drunk in the Spirit and experiencing overwhelming feelings of joy filled the airwaves. But controversy erupted almost immediately when the man who became the face of the holy laughter movement, South African evangelist Rodney Howard-Browne, was thrust onto the national stage. He was introduced to the church and the nation as the "Holy Ghost Bartender"[1] I personally heard him invite people to belly up to the bar and drink some new wine. Images of spiritually drunk charismatic Christians laughing uncontrollably were soon being broadcast on major news outlets and Christian programs everywhere. Christian leaders inside and outside the Charismatic movement reacted and condemned the disorderly behavior. But some famous word of faith and charismatic leaders hailed it as a great outpouring of the Spirit.

Randy Clark got the anointing from Rodney Howard-Browne in Tulsa and quickly stepped in front of the parade.[2] He became the face of the movement when the Toronto Blessing became a worldwide phenomenon. Both Clark and Howard-Browne talk more about revival, healing, and evangelism these days than they do holy laughter or other bizarre manifestations of the laughing revivals that made them famous. In fact, neither of them even mentions holy laughter on their websites. They have moved on to other things, and most charismatic believers have given them a pass. But what have they left in their wake? Did holy laughter open the door for some of the strange manifestations and extrabiblical experiences we hear so much about today? I think it did. The laughing revivals signaled a paradigm shift in the charismatic church that resulted in a disconnect from the Bible. A tragic mixture of flesh and spirit, truth and error, contaminated the charismatic stream. Many people say they were genuinely blessed, but the lasting fruit of the movements has generated a lot of questions and controversies.

Many respected leaders asked questions and raised concerns from the outset, but their questions often went unanswered and their warnings were ignored. Among well-known leaders who expressed concern were David Wilkerson, Steve Strang, and John Wimber. Wilkerson, the renowned author of the *Cross and the Switchblade* and pastor of Times Square Church, viewed the manifestations as fleshly at best and demonic at worst.[3] He blasted holy laughter in true Pentecostal prophetic form. Strang and Wimber had more reserved responses and appealed to reason.

The chaotic meetings were known for all manner of mayhem, spiritual drunkenness, and uncontrollable laughter. Manifestations of animal sounds like barking dogs, cackling hens, oinking pigs, crowing roosters, and roaring lions disturbed concerned leaders. Shockwaves shot through the church worldwide when it was learned that the leaders not only encouraged the bizarre behaviors, they claimed that they were manifestations of the Holy Spirit. It was quickly pointed out that while there had been weird manifestations in some of the great revivals of the past, leaders had not encouraged them; and they had certainly not attributed them to the Holy Spirit. But the leaders of the laughing revivals didn't back off; charismatics lined up on opposite sides of the issue and the division and controversy continue over twenty years after holy laughter broke out.

There had been reports of outbreaks of uncontrollable laughter in many parts of the USA and around the world for several years, but to my knowledge, it didn't become a worldwide phenomenon until its first name became "Holy" at Lakeland in 1993.

Famous word of faith leaders jumped in the holy laughter river in its early stages. They can still be seen in YouTube videos crawling around on all fours, laughing and carrying on with crowds of laughing spiritual drunkards.

Those who hoped it would be just a passing fad had their hopes dashed when in 1994 Randy Clark took the anointing north and transferred it to the leadership at the Airport Vineyard, where holy laughter became the Toronto Blessing. It then went viral to quickly spread to charismatic churches throughout the world. While charismatic believers everywhere testified of great impartations of joy, others looked on with disdain and lamented the reproach that such behaviors were bringing on the church. An army of evangelical apologists, amateur and professional, seized the opportunity to make "tongue talkers" look even crazier. My greatest concern was not arguing believers; it was the reaction of the lost. They laughed too—not with us, but at us.

Most honest believers would agree that the effect on the watching world was largely negative. The lost watch videos on the Internet and laugh at spiritual drunkards and human beings barking like dogs to this day. Shouldn't that deeply concern all of us? Paul the Apostle stressed that believers should always be careful to do everything possible to maintain a good testimony in the eyes of the world: "Be wise in the way you act toward those who are outside the Christian faith" (Col. 4:5, GW).

Was it wise for Christians to stagger around and fall like drunks during a worship service, laugh uncontrollably during a sermon, and bark like dogs and crow like roosters in a barnyard with secular journalists in the auditorium? Was it wise for controversial leaders to go on talk shows to defend such behaviors? In the age of video cameras, YouTube, and the Internet, was it wise for Christians to show blatant disregard for order and behave in a manner that caused the unsaved who view online videos and Facebook posts to wonder if we are mindless fools? No, it was not. How do I know? I have personally witnessed to countless people and have been compelled to convince them that Jesus, and most of His followers, have never barked like dogs or carried on the way people did in the laughing revivals. I had to field a lot of questions about bizarre behavior before I could even begin to share the gospel with them. I am weary of having to respond to questions about behaviors of flamboyant televangelists, money mongers, and charismatics gone weird before I can begin a conversation that points a lost person toward the cross.

Something from the Catch the Fire Toronto website, where the Toronto Blessing originated, reveals why the lost laughed and why believers divided over the issue. The following excerpt is from the history section of this site:

> The Toronto Blessing is a transferable anointing. In its most visible form it overcomes worshippers with outbreaks of laughter, weeping, groaning, shaking, falling, "drunkenness," and even behaviors that have been described as a "cross between a jungle and a farmyard." Of greater significance, however, are the changed lives.[4]

Jungle? Farmyard (or barnyard)? In a church? Holy laughter, Batman! I first beheld the barnyard and jungle behaviors personally at a large church south of St. Louis while doing research for a Modern Revivals class in a master's program with the Assemblies of God Theological Seminary. It took me all of a New York minute to realize that Rodney Howard-Browne seemed to have no regard for the order for which Paul appealed in 1 Corinthians 14. I was surrounded by charismatics gone weird, and it was evident that he was doing nothing to curb the behaviors; he was actually encouraging them. People fell throughout the service, laughed incessantly and uncontrollably, or cried, "I've fallen and I can't get up." An entire section to my right barked like dogs. They were answered by roaring lions from the left.

A woman in the row in front of me periodically crowed like a rooster, even moving her arms at her side like wings. Hysterical laughter broke out around her each time she did it. Those were less politically correct days, and I turned to a friend who had accompanied me and said, "Shouldn't she at least be cackling like a hen?" It was utter madness and mayhem; but not one word of correction or one call for order was issued during the entire service—even when it was all but impossible to hear the reading of a serious passage from Matthew chapter 24. I still have images of the chuckling "Holy Ghost Bartender" reading that sobering passage in that chaotic atmosphere. To this day, I don't understand how he could have done it.

I did some weird things in my hippie days with my stoned friends; but I never barked like a dog or crowed like a rooster—not even on the crazy streets of Isla Vista, California. I was appalled. I had just witnessed people showing total disregard for order and complete irreverence for the Bible. I had watched spiritual drunkards disrupt an entire service without being reproved. I had heard believers barking like dogs and a scantily clad woman crowing like a rooster. And Spirit-filled believers around the world insisted that such behaviors were a manifestation of the Holy Spirit! The argument is still alive and well over twenty years later. Honestly, do we need to wonder or argue whether such behaviors are a manifestation of a Spirit whose first name is Holy? Is there a hint anywhere in the New Testament that indicates that Jesus and the apostles ever acted like animals during a worship service? Can you in the farthest stretch of your imagination see Jesus acting like this—while a lost world is watching? I left the meeting and concluded, "This has to be a strong delusion."

Holy Laughter, Batman!

Something more than disorder or disrespect for the Bible troubled me upon leaving that meeting. I had seen this all before on more than one occasion—at least something uncannily similar to it. It had occurred during my hippie days in Southern California among Krishna devotees and followers of the "Giggling Guru," Maharishi Mahesh Yogi.[5] Such behaviors are common in Hindu gatherings in countries like India when the *Kundalini* spirit is activated and the "Divine Serpent of Truth" comes uncoiled.[6] It occurred among African villagers and sometimes in my crusades there. But even the simple African villagers—Christian and non-Christian—believed that people acting like animals was a demonic manifestation, sometimes as a result of a witchdoctor's curse. My practice had always been to cast demons out of such people. Dr. Lester Sumrall told me over breakfast that he had always treated it the same way. John Wimber often did too. But leaders of the laughing revivals were, without cracking a smile, defending such behaviors and attributing them to the Holy Spirit—and the world was watching. Holy laughter, Batman!

The behaviors that resemble activity in a jungle or on a barnyard, mentioned on the Catch the Fire Toronto site, are what most concerned John Wimber and other leaders. The position of the Vineyard Association of Churches was that such behaviors were manifestations of the flesh or demons. Wimber reminded leaders in Toronto in correspondence with them that the practice at the Anaheim Vineyard in the past had normally been to attempt to cast demons out of such people.[7]

But I think Wimber's concerns ran even deeper than

that. The problem with the laughing revivals was not just the nature of the manifestations. I honestly don't think it is necessary for mature believers, who are grounded in the Word of God, to discuss whether human beings making animal noises in a meeting are manifesting the Holy Spirit. We know they are not. There is no question that it was a problem—whether you believe the manifestations were just flesh unhinged or a devil. But even that was not the most serious problem. A deeper problem arose because people became more interested in seeking a manifestation than they were in seeking or manifesting Jesus. I am surprised that so much time has been spent simply talking about how bizarre and out of order the behaviors were. A deeper, underlying problem was that experience, not Jesus and not the Word, was at the center of the movement. Experience displaced Scripture. Behaviors and manifestations were not subjected to the Bible. The order for which Paul so clearly appealed in 1 Corinthians 14 was spurned. Few would question that the movements were deficient in sound teaching and instruction. Experience was emphasized and the Bible was not. Should we be surprised that things went a little weird? Should we be surprised that weirder things followed in their wake?

I have a copy of one of Wimber's letters which addresses the phenomena manifested in the Toronto Blessing. I also have some Vineyard Position Papers which deal with the subject.[8] A careful reading will reveal that Wimber's concern went even deeper than the problem presented in the last paragraph—the problem of allowing a movement to be built around experience. It even went deeper than the problems that develop when people become more interested in experiencing a manifestation than they are in manifesting Jesus. John Wimber was big on "doing the stuff" of ministry. What he saw happening in Toronto is that the seekers of impartations and manifestations weren't "doing the stuff" with the blessing they received. Leaders catered to their desire for experience and in so doing turned them into "meeting junkies" and "spiritual drunkards." They had to keep coming back for more and more. They lived for another meeting much like a junkie lives for another fix or a drunkard lives for another drink.

Night after night believers "bellied up to the bar" to drink some new wine, or got together in Toronto to "toke the Ghost." Churches became "party houses" and "bless me clubs." Believers left the party and if they reached out to the lost at all, they often talked more about their experiences than they did about Jesus. Experiences and manifestations became the focal point. Not much reverence was shown for the Holy Spirit. He was just there to dispense the "divine wine" or "heavenly weed" that produced the spiritual high. Now the New Mystics have taken it to another level: They don't just "sip the new wine" or "toke the Ghost;" they mimic cocaine users and "do lines of scripture." Is it OK to wonder if this could not be another Jesus and a different spirit? There is always great danger of deception when the Bible is subjugated to experience. It might be more correct to say that self became the center. Experience was exalted over truth and self was placed at the center—where God and His Word should always be.

So now we have experience exalted, God and His Word displaced, and self at the center. How did that affect outreach? Were people invited to meetings to hear the gospel?

Were they invited to come to hear about Jesus? Or were they invited to come and see what was going on? Were they invited to an experience? Now that might be alright to a point, if the experience is clearly biblical. But what if that is questionable? What if experience has gone weird and wild and leaders refuse to subject it to Scripture? What will be the long-term fruit of doing that? I can answer that question by simply suggesting something for you to do: Look around you. What kind of lasting fruit do you see from the laughing revivals? Are you happy with the condition of the church today? The Global Awakening website says that the revival birthed in Toronto was the greatest revival of the last half of the twentieth century.[9] Holy, astronomical claim, Batman! Do you believe it: Greater than the Jesus movement? Greater than the Charismatic movement? Does the fruit validate that claim?

There is a lot of lasting fruit—good fruit—from the Jesus and Charismatic movements. It has stood the test of time. Shouldn't a man stand around and inspect fruit a little longer before proclaiming the revival with his name attached to it the greatest movement of the last half of the previous century? What about the fruit? Time will tell—or has it already told? Is there a reason why the leaders of the laughing revivals seem to be distancing themselves from the movements and bizarre manifestations that made them famous? Is there a reason holy laughter and the other strange manifestations they once called manifestations of the Holy Spirit are not even mentioned on their websites? Could it be that the respected leaders who raised concerns were right after all?

Did you ever listen to any of the people who got the

"anointing" or the "blessing" witness to the lost? I did. I had to follow people around and observe them; it was part of my research for the Modern Revivals course I mentioned earlier. Listening to them witness was a real trip. You should have heard the conversations and observed the behavior in restaurants after the Holy Ghost parties. I developed greater appreciation for waitresses back then that remains to this day. If I had been the lost person some of them "witnessed" to, you would have had to pay me to go to a meeting at their church—and I'm not sure you could have paid me enough. Why do charismatic believers keep doing things that make lost people wonder if we are all from "Weirdsville?"

The drunken laughers and barkers I observed didn't talk much about Jesus: they talked about manifestations. They were so jazzed about them, they didn't notice the bewildered expressions on the faces of people being "witnessed" to. Reading their expressions, I surmised that most lost people thought the manifestations were more super *weird* than supernatural.

You may be wondering: Why bring up holy laughter and the Toronto Blessing so many years after it hit? For the same reason my tax dollars are helping clean up a nuclear waste site that has been near my home for many years; there is still fallout from it. Division happened the moment holy laughter hit the Charismatic movement. Bizarre behaviors like spiritual drunkenness, uncontrollable hysterical laughing, and animal sounds during meetings had people lining up on opposite sides of the issue from the beginning. Some claimed the manifestations were born of the Spirit; others said they were at best fleshly, and at worst demonic. I would like to forget what lies behind and put holy laughter to bed—but it is not sleepy yet.

The laughing revivals sparked controversy and division in the Charismatic movement worldwide. Many people claimed to be blessed but leaders were troubled that so much reproach was being brought on the church. The world watched and laughed and evangelical Christians concluded that charismatics were as crazy as some apologists portrayed them to be. The warnings and concerns of leaders inside and outside the Charismatic movement were not heeded. Again, the most troubling thing to leaders who preferred to stay a little closer to the Bible were the unscriptural behaviors like animal sounds coupled with a total disregard for order. They were not concerned simply because people were barking and cackling and crowing, etc., but that such behaviors were encouraged—and even called manifestations of the Holy Spirit.

That is what made these movements and leaders so different from those of the past. There had been weird manifestations in great revivals of history, but leaders had typically discouraged and tried to curb them. Now they were encouraged and even attributed to the Holy Spirit. The Vineyard Association was very open to supernatural phenomena; but it had always viewed people making animal noises as being in the flesh or demonized. As mentioned earlier, before the Toronto Blessing, Vineyard ministers attempted to restrain such behavior, sometimes by casting demons out of people. It seemed incredulous that what had been previously been laid at the devil's door was now being called a manifestation of the Spirit. And it was more disturbing that so few leaders in charismatic circles spoke out against it. Thank God for those who did.

I mentioned earlier that David Wilkerson, Steve Strang, and John Wimber were among those who raised concerns and issued warnings early on. Wilkerson blasted it. At times he was overcome with weeping as he talked about the manifestations. He lamented that they were making the Holy Spirit look like a fool. Wimber and Strang appealed to both Scripture and reason. They addressed concerns and warned of possible negative repercussions. But leaders of the laughing revivals refused to subject their meetings to a scriptural test. They discounted the warnings and forged ahead with little regard for order. Much of what concerned leaders warned might happen has now come to pass.

Steve Strang is founder and CEO of Charisma Media (formerly Strang Communications), a Christian multimedia company. It publishes magazines such as *Charisma*, *Ministry Today*, and others and books through several book groups including Charisma House and Creation House, the company that is publishing this book and two others I have recently written.[10] Strang raised concerns earlier than most. He demonstrated a lot of levelheadedness in the way he responded to some of the behaviors taking place in Toronto. I still have articles from *Charisma Magazine* in my files that date back to the turbulent era when holy laughter was spreading in American, Canadian and European churches.

In the early days of the Toronto Blessing, Strang attended a meeting at the Airport Vineyard and was slain in the Spirit. Leaders there hoped he would endorse the movement. In a statement which was published not long after the meeting in Toronto, he urged caution. "Am I endorsing what I saw and experienced in Toronto? No, because I still don't understand much of it. Similar manifestations have occurred in past revivals; but I believe an experience should also be established in the Word of God."[11] Strang went on to express concern that people who didn't experience the manifestations might come under pressure and be tempted to fake them. I have seen his "prophecy" fulfilled in many nations.

I remember how much Strang's reasoned response helped me during the early days of the holy laughter outbreak. Pastors and friends in the ministry were pressuring me to "get freed up," "belly up to the bar," and "jump in the river." I refrained because I also questioned whether much of what was taking place had precedence in Scripture. Strang's statement that he believed an experience should also be established in the Word of God helped me stand firm on my convictions. I never did jump in the holy laughter river, and I have no regrets.

David Wilkerson was grieved not only by its effects on American churches, but over its influence around the world. I have received his newsletter every month nonstop since 1972.[12] I have correspondence from the 1990s in which he issued warnings about the laughing revivals. He urged Christians to weep over lost souls and to cry out for millions of unborn children who were being aborted if we wanted to see true revival. He lamented that while the pressures of life had become so unbearable that hell-bound sinners cried themselves to sleep, charismatics found relief by barking like dogs and laughing uncontrollably. He consistently preached that real joy would come when the lost were saved as a result of authentic revival born out of repentance and prayer.

Wilkerson, like many other seasoned leaders, was of the opinion that Satan often brings counterfeit revivals at a time when God's people are desperate for a fresh touch of His Spirit. The repentance and prayer that could produce real revival are neglected when impatient believers, who are looking for a shortcut to revival, embrace a counterfeit. In short, he thought that charismatics had the order messed up: joy and laughter should follow prayer and weeping that produces authentic revival in which souls are saved.[13] "They that sow in tears shall reap in joy. He that goeth forth and weepeth, bearing precious seed, shall doubtless come again with rejoicing, bringing his sheaves with him" (Ps. 126:5–6, KJV).

While many charismatic pastors and churches ran to the security of the extremely orderly seeker-sensitive movement, I went deeper into Pentecost. I was grieved over what was happening in the Charismatic movement, and I was disturbed that more leaders were not willing to speak out publicly to warn against the dangers of intermingling with the confusion surrounding the bizarre behaviors of the laughing revivals. But I rejected the confusion and disorder, not the Spirit who brought order out of chaos at Creation.

I tried to help churches that were fighting fallout—some which I had established; but I was never once tempted to suggest restriction or rejection of the moving of the Holy Spirit as a solution. I ran to Him, not away from Him. I found strength in God's presence in places like Times

Square Church and in meetings with B. H. Clendennen, one of the true Pentecostal pioneers of the last century. My refusal to sacrifice the authentic in the midst of mayhem eventually led to a great blessing. Clendennen asked me to serve as director of the School of Christ International for the continent of Africa. I had the privilege of ministering for years at the forefront of a great soul winning revival that blazed across Africa—where we viewed barking dogs and crowing roosters as believers had from the early days of missionary activity there. We treated them as confused people who needed to exercise self-control and restrain their flesh; and in some cases, as John Wimber had done in early years at the Anaheim Vineyard, we cast demons out of them.

A message brought by David Wilkerson at Times Square Church in 2000, and also in Moscow where I ministered numerous times from 1996 through 2003, further confirmed my convictions. He described a pastor he knew who had not been able to preach for weeks because he was overcome with hysterical laughter whenever he entered the pulpit.[14] Wilkerson went on to lament the manifestations occurring including the behavior of a well-known word of faith leader who stuck out his tongue and hissed like a snake as he walked among laughing people at his conference. He continued, "I don't see anything to laugh about. I can't laugh....I can't laugh when they make the Holy Ghost look like a fool."[15] At this point in the sermon he was overcome with a truly holy response to such behaviors—weeping. He tried for a few moments to fight back tears but finally left the pulpit to pray, unable to continue preaching. I believe the message is available from

World Challenge. A clip of the video from Moscow has circulated widely on the Internet.

There is no question that Wilkerson, the well-known author of *The Cross and the Switchblade* and founder of Times Square Church, was deeply disturbed over the bizarre behaviors long before that message in Moscow. He issued warnings everywhere. He, like many others, was concerned that spirits, not just flesh, were invading churches. In its October 1999 issue, *Charisma Magazine* ran excerpts from a sermon delivered at Times Square Church earlier that year in which Wilkerson blasted "prosperity doctrines [and] 'holy laughter.'"[16] In a stinging rebuke, he disparaged them for what he considered foolish, unscriptural behavior: "He also told his parishioners to stay away from evangelist Rodney Howard-Browne's Good News New York crusade...."[17]

Wilkerson went on to level "blasphemy charges at the prosperity doctrines...saying, 'It's an American gospel invented and spread by rich American evangelists and pastors.'"[18] He referred to reprehensible behavior by two famous leaders of the Word of Faith movement and even leveled blasphemy charges at one of them."[19] He expressed revulsion over the manifestations associated with the holy laughter and Toronto Blessing movements: "'I weep when I see these videos that are sent to me from all over the country. Whole groups of bodies jerking out of control, falling on the floor, laughing hysterically, staggering around like drunkards,' Wilkerson said. 'Anything that cannot be found in Scripture has to be rejected outright—totally rejected.'"[20]

I mentioned earlier that I am raising issues and

rehashing sermons that were preached years ago for the same reason that my tax dollars are helping fund a multimillion dollar nuclear waste cleanup project near my home—the fallout from elements that contaminated the environment over fifty years ago still pose a threat today. I just returned from conducting evangelistic crusades in Costa Rica with churches I helped establish there in the 1980s. They are still affected by holy laughter fallout and have experienced the pain predicted by Wimber. Holy laughter caused divisions there as it did in other countries where I have ministered.

I had to deal with problems stemming from it with many leaders who attended my crusades and schools in Africa. African pastors were confused by what they saw on programs of word of faith televangelists when satellite television became available there in the 1990s. Rodney Howard-Browne appeared with key leaders of the faith movement on programs at that time. A video with he and Kenneth Copeland laughing and "dueling" in tongues was particularly disturbing to leaders who attended our schools. It created a lot of confusion in Africa. But leaders there were most concerned about people acting like animals. They had dealt with witchcraft all their lives, and a person acting like an animal was almost always thought to be under a witchdoctor's curse or demonized. They were perplexed that manifestations they had always treated as demonic were being attributed to the Holy Spirit by famous American preachers who they looked up to. Few American charismatics realize how much confusion and division were caused by the holy laughter and Toronto Blessing movements in other countries.

The argument that leaders thought to be drunk on the Day of Pentecost were doing the same things as those in modern movements doesn't hold water. We weren't there to observe the behavior of the believers on the Day of Pentecost. However, upon careful reading of the account, I am certain that Peter and the other apostles did not behave as did the leaders of the modern laughing revivals. No thinking person who reads Peter's sermon in Acts chapter 2 would even entertain such a thought.

Much of what I observed in the laughing revivals could not have been the fruit of the Holy Spirit. Given the frequent use of "uncontrollable" to describe behaviors, I believe it is worth noting again that one of the fruit of the Spirit is self control (Gal. 5:22–23). At best, many of the manifestations were fleshly and emotional. At worst, many of them were produced by another spirit or spirits—like the seducing spirits of a Hindu deity. I can assure you on the authority of Scripture, and on an understanding of the culture and moral code of the New Testament era, men and women were not flopping around together on the ground while laughing uncontrollably; and I can assure you that Spirit-filled believers were not barking like dogs or clucking like chickens. I have absolutely no doubt that they were listening—not laughing—as Peter delivered the convicting message that resulted in three thousand converts on the Day of Pentecost. And by noting the organization and clarity of his presentation, I can assure you that his mind was not filled with the fog of "drunken glory," his preaching was not laced with laughter, and he was not drooling like a drunkard as he preached the powerful and sobering message that caused hearers to cry out, "What must we do?" Their cries were followed by repentance, not hysterical laughter and animal noises. It is ludicrous to compare the manifestations of the laughing revivals to anything that took place on the Day of Pentecost.

CHAPTER 9

THE CATASTROPHE OF COMPROMISE

IS THE WESTERN church so compromised that it has lost the power to influence culture? Are compromised believers in danger of becoming salt that has lost its savor (Matt. 5:13)? Is it truly possible that nearly the whole train is off the tracks? It wouldn't be the first time. It happened in the days of Noah. The population of the whole world had departed from truth and righteousness. Noah and his family were the only ones who escaped judgment (Gen. 6:5–8).

It happened again in the days of Elijah. Many true prophets of the Lord had been slain by King Ahab and Queen Jezebel. Elijah had to hide at a widow's house where he was supernaturally sustained by God; and Obadiah, an official in the royal court, hid one hundred prophets in caves. Elijah was lonely when he challenged the false prophets on Mt. Carmel. It was eight hundred fifty to one—Elijah against all the false prophets that dined at the wicked queen's table (1 Kings 18). Nearly the whole train was off the tracks.

It happened again in the days of Jeremiah. As you read his confrontational, in-your-face statements, it won't sound much like the popular preachers of our age—but remember; this is God talking:

> My people are fools; they do not know me. They are senseless children: they have no understanding. They are skilled in doing evil; they know not how to do good.... Go up and down the streets of Jerusalem, look around and consider, search through her squares. If you can find but one person who deals honestly and seeks the truth, I will forgive this city.
> —Jeremiah 4:22; 5:1

Why did it happen? Why was the whole nation in such a backslidden state? The problem was primarily the fault of compromising leaders:

> "Woe to the shepherds who are destroying and scattering the sheep of my pasture!" declares the Lord. Therefore this is what the Lord, the God of Israel, says to the shepherds who tend my people: "Because you have scattered my flock and driven them away and have not bestowed care on them, I will bestow punishment on you for the evil you have done," declares the Lord.... The land is full of adulterers; because of the curse the land lies parched and the pastures in the wilderness are withered. The prophets follow an evil course and use their power unjustly. Both prophet and priest are godless; even in my temple I find their wickedness," declares the Lord.... "Do not listen to what the prophets are prophesying to you; they fill you with false hopes. They speak visions from their own minds, not from

> the mouth of the LORD....I did not send these prophets, yet they have run with their message; I did not speak to them, yet they have prophesied. But if they had stood in my council, they would have proclaimed my words to my people and would have turned them from their evil ways and from their evil deeds.
> —JEREMIAH 23:1–2, 10–11, 16, 21–22

History repeats itself. Can any honest student of Scripture deny that there are striking similarities between the condition of modern America and ancient Israel in the days of Jeremiah? We have experienced a moral free fall. Many of the values that made our nation great have been discarded. Truth is being trampled in the streets as in the days of Isaiah, Jeremiah, and Ezekiel:

> Justice is turned back, And righteousness stands afar off; For truth is fallen in the street, And equity cannot enter. So truth fails, And he who departs from evil makes himself a prey.
> —ISAIAH 59:14–15, NKJV

The problems in the days of Isaiah, Jeremiah, and Ezekiel were primarily caused by compromised preachers who were more concerned about prosperity and popularity than preaching the truth. Their compromise led to catastrophe. Most of the nation was backslidden, and prophets were not calling the people of God to repentance. In the face of impending judgment, false prophets continued preaching peace and prosperity. Is it any different today? When is the last time you heard a seeker-sensitive pastor or a prosperity preacher confront sin or call people to repentance? Are the wealthy faith and prosperity preachers of our day any different than the false prophets of Jeremiah's day? Can the charismatic leaders, who encourage believers to laugh uncontrollably, bark like dogs, "sip the new wine," and "toke the Ghost," turn the tide? Will self-appointed, title-loving apostles, or the prophets with a positive personal word for nearly everyone they meet return the nation to godliness? Is there any hope that leaders who preach love without convictions can impact the culture? Can the recently resurrected message of cheap grace produce repentance—or has it actually increased the danger of derailment by emphasizing grace to the point of lawlessness? The trend should alarm sincere believers—especially those who have knowledge of the first century heresy of antinomianism, which simply translated means against or without law. This heresy creates a casual attitude toward sin that always results in a moral train wreck.

God's people wouldn't listen to Jeremiah. They preferred the pleasant, positive false prophets who preached peace and prosperity. They didn't wake up until the invaders Jeremiah had warned about were ravaging the land and carrying away captives to Babylon. Nearly the whole train was off the tracks, but they didn't realize it until it was too late. They didn't realize it because they wouldn't listen to the convicting preaching of a lonely lover of truth. They mocked and persecuted Jeremiah. They didn't want him disturbing their comfort or ruining their fantasy of the good life. They tried to ignore his irritating messages filled with warnings; they did all they could to shut him up. He agonized and prayed with tears but the train wreck could not be averted. Why? God's people were deceived by doctrines of demons. They listened to prosperity seeking false prophets and rejected Jeremiah's warnings. History reveals that they listened to the wrong message and they suffered horribly for their lack of love for the truth.

Could it be that the same thing is happening in America? Many modern Christians seem to prefer watered-down, pleasant sounding sermons to messages preached with conviction and filled with truth. The shallow sermons of popular television celebrities are preferred over the heartfelt preaching of God-fearing pastors. We should learn from the past. God was not with the majority; He was hanging out with a weeping prophet who loved the truth. That is why nobody remembers the names of the false prophets but parents are still naming children after Jeremiah. Those who love the Word of God have no difficulty understanding what is happening in the modern church. It has happened before. They know that preachers, more than politicians, are responsible for the moral landslide in this former God-fearing nation.

Repentance could bring revival. The train could get back on the tracks. Deceived believers could come out of the fog by simply reading the first chapter of Romans with eyes wide open. Consider the following rather lengthy passage with Bible history as a backdrop:

> The wrath of God is being revealed from heaven against all the godlessness and wickedness of people, who suppress the truth by their wickedness, since what may be known about God is plain to them, because God has made it plain to them. For since the creation of the world God's invisible qualities—his

eternal power and divine nature—have been clearly seen, being understood from what has been made, so that people are without excuse. For although they knew God, they neither glorified him as God nor gave thanks to him, but their thinking became futile and their foolish hearts were darkened.... Therefore God gave them over in the sinful desires of their hearts to sexual impurity for the degrading of their bodies with one another. They exchanged the truth about God for a lie, and worshiped and served created things rather than the Creator—who is forever praised. Amen. Because of this, God gave them over to shameful lusts. Even their women exchanged natural sexual relations for unnatural ones. In the same way the men also abandoned natural relations with women and were inflamed with lust for one another. Men committed shameful acts with other men, and received in themselves the due penalty for their error. Furthermore, just as they did not think it worthwhile to retain the knowledge of God, so God gave them over to a depraved mind, so that they do what ought not to be done. They have become filled with every kind of wickedness, evil, greed and depravity. They are full of envy, murder, strife, deceit and malice. They are gossips, slanderers, God-haters, insolent, arrogant and boastful; they invent ways of doing evil; they disobey their parents; they have no understanding, no fidelity, no love, no mercy. Although they know God's righteous decree that those who do such things deserve death, they not only continue to do these very things but also approve of those who practice them.

—ROMANS 1:18–21, 24–32

The following verses clearly reveal the reason for the present condition of the American church and culture:

> The coming of the lawless one will be in accordance with how Satan works. He will use all sorts of displays of power through signs and wonders that serve the lie, and all the ways that wickedness deceives those who are perishing. They perish because they refused to love the truth and so be saved. For this reason God sends them a powerful delusion so that they will believe the lie and so that all will be condemned who have not believed the truth but have delighted in wickedness.
> —2 Thessalonians 2:9–12

I am using a lot of scripture in this chapter. If you are still reading, I assume you may be able to digest more than others who didn't come this far on the journey. I am also including numerous verses and passages to counteract the current trend of preaching popular messages with little scriptural support. Have you noticed how often so called "word preachers" do not insert much of the Word in their sermons? The powerful delusion of which Paul warned us has come because so few today preach "the whole counsel of God" (Acts 20:27, NKJV).

I stated earlier that emphasizing one truth to the neglect of others can lead to full-blown heresy. It can also lead to the kind of delusion that so concerned the great apostle. A delusion is a false idea or belief. The modern church is filled with them because of a plethora of preachers who handle the Word of God without reverence or integrity. They select favorite passages that support their beliefs.

They avoid equally inspired ones that clarify or correct their imbalanced doctrine. They are the teachers referenced in 2 Timothy 4:3: "For the time will come when they will not endure sound doctrine; but after their own lusts shall they heap to themselves teachers, having itching ears" (KJV). Deluded believers prefer teachers who are willing to preach what they want to hear and scratch them where they itch over those who preach what they need to hear.

Such preachers have sold out to the spirit of delusion. The market where preachers are bought and sold is always open. The devil is relentless in his efforts to tempt a sincere preacher to compromise. Money is no issue in this market and the moment Satan discovers a preacher has a price, buyers appear. He has bought many who wouldn't give up under pressure or persecution. After fighting a good fight on a vicious field of battle, they caved in to something much more dangerous than open confrontation with the enemy—subtle deception. In a moment of weakness, they sold out for popularity and prosperity. If you are a lover of truth who hasn't sold out, you have earned an awesome responsibility and a great honor—standing for truth in an age of compromise, deception, and delusion.

Is there hope for the modern church? Can we get the train back on the tracks? Can we prevail against seducing spirits and doctrines of demons?" Countless preachers in sermons on the end times have said that this is the age of the Laodicean church. There are many similarities; but, as we look at them, I want to remind you that Jesus held out hope of recovery even for the compromised church of Laodicea. A little further along we will read His message to believers in Laodicea with the modern church in mind. The future of the church in America depends on how believers like us respond to the words of the Master to the churches of Asia over two millenniums ago. How we respond to the message to the Laodiceans may well determine whether we continue in delusion or repent and see a true, heaven-sent revival.

The similarities between Laodicea and the modern church in America, and much of the Western world, are apparent to any honest reader. The commitment and dedication of the Laodiceans were both in question. Jesus described them as lukewarm. They had lost their passion. A loss of passion is always accompanied by a lack of intimacy and a departure from our first love. Believers in this condition have lost their focus; they have become distracted; they have lost their burden for the lost and their sense of urgency to fulfill the Great Commission. Lukewarm believers are lethargic. They have lost their enthusiasm for the most exciting activity a human being can experience—following Jesus. His reaction to their condition should arrest our attention: He said that it would be better to be cold than lukewarm. The lukewarm state of believers disgusted Him. He said basically, "Get over it or I will spit you out of my mouth."

Why is there such danger in being lukewarm? It causes believers to become bored. It creates emptiness that demands to be filled. It causes people to lose sight of priorities and invest themselves in things less important. It causes believers to pick up the remote control instead of a Bible; it causes them to watch television for three hours and pray for three minutes. It causes them to look for shortcuts to revival and engage in all manner of foolishness.

Lukewarmness results in a spiritual void that leaves the believer powerless to influence an ungodly culture. In fact, lukewarm believers often become victims of the culture. How is that possible? Some become so comfortable in an ungodly culture they are absorbed by it. In their apathy, they treat the world system like a misunderstood friend instead of an enemy. Even worse, if the downward spiral into lukewarmness is not interrupted, they will not only make peace with their "misunderstood friend"—they will be entertained by him. To the lukewarm believer the world becomes a playground, not a battleground. Such believers willingly bow down to the great god of entertainment that helps them deal with their boredom and forget the danger of their condition.

You may have heard the story of the bullfrog that was boiled in a big pot of water. He was first dropped into a pot of ice water and he jumped right out. Then he was dropped into a pot of hot water and had the same reaction. Finally, he was placed in a pot of lukewarm water and he started swimming around in it. He became so comfortable he got sleepy—so sleepy he didn't notice the water getting hotter. The researchers who conducted the experiment gradually turned up the heat and cooked the poor frog one degree at a time. By the time he woke up to the danger, it was too late. He no longer had the strength to jump out of the pot. This is the danger—and the result—of lukewarmness. Delusion won't just deceive you; if you wait too long to get out, it will cook you.

I learned shortly after receiving my pilot's license how being off course just a degree can cause big problems a little farther down the line. I learned it the hard way and faced a lot of embarrassment because of it. My flight instructor told me over and over again not to get lazy. He taught me to believe the instruments when I had no visibility but to always double check when it was clear by charting my course and noting visual checkpoints along the way. I ignored my training one Sunday while flying a few hundred miles from Missouri to Indiana for a meeting.

I set my navigational instrument to an FM station emitting a signal from near the airport to which I wanted to fly and listened to music along the way. I didn't bother checking visual references en route. The flight was non-eventful and I easily spotted the airport just outside the city. I landed without a hitch and was surprised that no one was there to pick me. The meeting where I was to speak was scheduled to begin in less than an hour. I called the pastor to see if someone was on the way to pick me up and he said, "I am here. Just look over by the ticket counter."

I looked and assured him that he was not *here*. He then asked, "What is the name of the airport you are at?" I gave him the name from the chart I had not followed and he said, "You are not at that airport. Ask someone the name of the airport." I thought, "This is ridiculous!" But to humor him, I asked. The answer was not what I wanted to hear. It was a different airport—twenty miles from the one near the church where I was supposed to land. With my lazy navigation I had drifted slightly off course and that slight error over several hours of flying became a twenty mile mistake. When I saw the airport in my flight path so close to my destination, I simply assumed it was the right one.

The pastor didn't think much of my piloting skills. And he wasn't too concerned about my feelings either. He didn't introduce me as a missionary-evangelist who had preached around the world. He introduced me as the bumbling pilot-preacher who had landed at the wrong airport. He laughed as he told the whole congregation what I had done. He even used the opportunity to teach briefly on the importance of checking our course and making periodic adjustments on our journey toward heaven.

Like me on that infamous flight, I think the modern church has become a bit too careless in its navigation. We too quickly embrace extrabiblical revelations without checking the chart. If we do not become more careful, we may soon discover that we have been taken far off course. We need to check the chart and make sure that the "extra" in extrabiblical is biblical. We need to follow Paul's advice to Timothy: "Study to shew thyself approved unto God, a workman that needeth not to be ashamed, rightly dividing the word of truth" (2 Tim. 2:15, KJV). A little more study and reflection might save us a world of trouble. Upon more diligent examination, we may discover that we are a degree or two off course. Over time that could lead to serious error. The prudent thing to do is to make adjustments now—before we go any farther down the road.

That is what Jesus gave the Laodiceans an opportunity to do: make adjustments by repenting and fanning the flames of commitment and dedication. The Word of God is given to help us see where we are in relation to the course God has laid out for us. The Spirit deals with our hearts when we begin to drift off course. If we are sensitive to His warnings, He will help us make the necessary corrections to get back on track. Many modern movements, especially those being led by spiritual specialists, could experience revolutionary change if they would heed the warnings of the Holy Spirit. The faith, love, and grace specialists could do a lot to get the train back on the tracks by being willing to embrace the whole counsel of God instead of insisting on emphasizing their favorite selected passages. Emphasizing one, or a few, favorite truths to the neglect of others will take a person way off course. It may eventually land you at an airport run by seducing spirits that traffic in doctrines of demons.

We should be cautious about flying too far into extrabiblical territory. Staying close to the written Word is our greatest safeguard. We need to get over our love affair with personal words of prophecy and renew our vows to the written Word of God. It must always be our compass. Passages like 2 Timothy 3:15 must be held close to our hearts: "All Scripture is God-breathed and is useful for teaching, rebuking, correcting and training in righteousness, so that the servant of God may be thoroughly equipped for every good work" (2 Tim. 3:16–17). I like the way the New King James Version translates these verses: "All Scripture is given by inspiration of God, and is profitable for doctrine, for reproof, for correction, for instruction in righteousness, that the man of God may be complete, thoroughly equipped for every good work."

Notice that the passage begins with the words "All scripture is profitable." Every godly preacher believes that when God says "all" He means "all." We should not run from, hide from, or neglect any passage of Scripture. If we have integrity, we will refuse to live with the kind of deluded thinking that makes a man think he has the right to continually select his favorite subject and pass on the rest. Preaching nothing but positive scriptures will lead you to a negative destination.

Even a car depends on both the negative and positive to start and run. A battery can't function without both a negative and positive pole. With just one it would be without power. The same is true in the Christian life. Trying to run on nothing but the positive side of love, faith, or grace will eventually leave you powerless and vulnerable to seducing spirits and doctrines of demons. Disaster is just a little ways down the road for those who refuse to handle the Word of God with integrity by esteeming "all" scripture. Failing to preach the whole counsel of God will lead to certain disaster. There is always catastrophe on the other side of compromise.

If you don't believe it, take a history lesson from the Laodiceans. Here are the words of Jesus to the church at Laodicea: A modern church infested with seducing spirits and doctrines of demons would be wise to heed them.

> To the angel of the church in Laodicea write: These are the words of the Amen, the faithful and true witness, the ruler of God's creation. I know your deeds, that you are neither cold nor hot. I wish you were either one or the other! So, because you are lukewarm—neither hot nor cold—I am about to spit you out of my mouth. You say, "I am rich; I have acquired wealth and do not need a thing." But you do not realize that you are wretched, pitiful, poor, blind and naked. I counsel you to buy from me gold refined in the fire, so you can become rich;

and white clothes to wear, so you can cover your shameful nakedness; and salve to put on your eyes, so you can see.
—Revelation 3:14–18

Earlier we saw that Jesus had a contention with the Laodiceans because they had become lukewarm in their relationship with Him. Another contention He had with them begins in verse 17. They were focused on the wrong kind of riches. They were materially prosperous. They thought they were wealthy. Jesus had a different opinion. He told them they were "wretched, pitiful, poor, blind and naked." He prefaced His description with a statement that should have struck fear in their hearts. In essence He told them, "You are really messed up but you don't even realize it." That is the power and danger of delusion.

He told them they needed to trade in their worldly wealth for true, spiritual riches: "gold refined in the fire." He told them they needed to exchange their expensive clothes for white robes of righteousness. Finally, He again emphasized their spiritual blindness by counseling them to buy from Him eye salve that would enable them to see. This is shocking. How is it that they did not realize their true condition before God?

Is it possible that a modern church fixated on material prosperity is in the same condition? Is it possible that a gospel that puts more emphasis on prosperity than preaching the cross is a perverted gospel? Have we become deluded by seducing spirits which travel with wealthy preachers who wear expensive clothes and possess a lot of spiritually unrefined gold? Would we be wise to revisit

Jesus' call to discipleship and hear again His warning to those who fail to properly respond to it?

> "Then he called the crowd to him along with his disciples and said: "Whoever wants to be my disciple must deny themselves and take up their cross and follow me. For whoever wants to save their life will lose it, but whoever loses their life for me and for the gospel will save it. What good is it for someone to gain the whole world, yet forfeit their soul? Or what can anyone give in exchange for their soul?"
> —MARK 8:34–37

The faith and prosperity gospel has been popular in America since the early days of the Charismatic movement. Many of its leaders have grown wealthy while many of their supporters have become impoverished. Its influence is so insidious that it has spread to affect the thinking of Christians who haven't even bought into it. Sadly, many lost people have also been negatively affected by it. I have witnessed to countless people who have never attended a church; yet they have opinions about Christians that hinder their receptivity to the gospel. It's interesting to me that many of their opinions about church were formed without ever attending a church service. They formed them from watching preachers on Christian television. I have heard this statement over and over again: "All preachers care about is your money." Where did they get that idea? The answer is obvious, but I will answer in my own words. They got it from greedy televangelists and big shot network owners who generously pay seed-seekers to help them with their telethons.

With Jesus' words to the Laodiceans fresh on our minds, allow me to pose another question: How rich is the preacher who has driven lost souls away from Jesus with a materialistic misrepresentation of the gospel? Is all the material wealth he could amass in a lifetime of prosperity preaching worth as much as one lost soul? It is not if you believe what Jesus said in Mark 8:34–37. How many lost people have been turned off to the gospel because, in a time of need when they were searching for help, they tuned into a Christian station and encountered a prosperity preacher talking about money instead of Jesus?

Any honest Christian who truly believes Jesus' words to the Laodiceans knows that we are laboring under a serious delusion in America. Word of faith preachers have made material prosperity the status symbol of faith. Everyone with faith and the right confession, who sows generous financial seeds, is assured that they will reap an abundant harvest and prosper. But the vast majority do not. The ones reaping the greatest benefit are the seed-seekers themselves. Many of them have become very wealthy—or have they? I wonder how many will one day hear Jesus say, "You are wretched, poor, pitiful, blind and naked—and you didn't even realize it. I tried to tell you but you wouldn't listen."

I decided years ago that I didn't want the brand of faith being marketed by prosperity preachers in America. I have to admit that in terms of dollars that decision cost me dearly: But did it truly cost me? The answer depends on perspective. I had the opportunity to rise higher in the movement, but I didn't play by the rules. It was understood that to get to the next level you had to sow seed into it. For those who need an explanation, that means I had to give offerings to someone higher up the food chain if I wanted to rise to their level. It was also explained to me that to come up higher I would have to part with friends at my present level. I chose to do neither.

I opted to look for role models in the Bible instead of on television. My favorite became the Apostle Paul. My goal is to obtain even a fraction of the faith and love he possessed: faith and love that will pour itself out for the gospel's sake and gladly spend itself to the point of suffering and sacrifice in the pursuit of lost souls. I want the faith of the New Testament—faith which embraces the cross not only for what it does for me but for what it does to me. I want the kind of faith that is willing to deny itself, take up its cross daily and walk in the steps of the most faith-filled Man who ever visited the planet. I want faith that will mature to the point that I will someday be able to say in sincerity and raw truth, "I am crucified with Christ: nevertheless I live; yet not I, but Christ liveth in me: and the life which I now live in the flesh I live by the faith of the Son of God, who loved me, and gave himself for me" (Gal. 2:20, KJV).

Is there hope for a church that has allowed and even propagated delusion? Is there hope for preachers who have perverted the true Bible message of faith and used another gospel to make merchandise of the people of God? Is there hope for preachers who push grace to the point of lawlessness and pass out licenses to sin? Is there hope for preachers who are all sugar and no salt? Is there hope for preachers who recognized the delusion but remained silent in order to avoid controversy? There is if they can find their voices. There is if they can hear what Jesus is saying to the churches. There is if they will repent and use their faith to buy the true riches Jesus offered the Laodiceans. And if they refuse? Hell is probably holding reservations in their names.

Jesus is merciful. His rebuke to the deluded Laodicean believers flowed from a heart of love. The rebuke was followed by an appeal and an invitation to come out of the fog. There is always hope for those who are willing to humble themselves, repent, and open the door.

> Those whom I love I rebuke and discipline. So be earnest and repent. Here I am! I stand at the door and knock. If anyone hears my voice and opens the door, I will come in and eat with that person, and they with me. To the one who is victorious, I will give the right to sit with me on my throne, just as I was victorious and sat down with my Father on his throne. Whoever has ears, let them hear what the Spirit says to the churches.
> —REVELATION 3:19–22

NOTES

Chapter 1
Subtle and Seducing Influences

1. *Merriam-Webster Online*, s.v. "dilute," http://www.merriam-webster.com/dictionary/dilute (accessed August 26, 2015).
2. Ron Sutton and Ryan Sutton, *Sacred Fire: Why Don't We Try Pentecost One More Time* (Lake Mary, FL: Creation House, 2015), 68–69.

Chapter 2
Spiritual Specialists

1. Ibid., 60.

Chapter 3
Brother Love's Traveling Salvation Show

1. Neil Diamond, "Brother Love's Travelling Salvation Show," Uni Records, a division of MCA's Universal Studios, Los Angeles, 1969.
2. Barbara Harris Whitfield, "Kundalini-101: The Energy and How It Works," *Kundalini Research Network* (blog), June 1, 2011, http://krnweb.blogspot.com/2011/06/kundalini-101-energy-and-how-it-works.html (accessed August 25, 2015).
3. Judaizers were Pharisees, and those influenced by them, who were converted to Christianity but held on to their legalism. They added works to the gospel of

salvation by grace through faith and tried to impose their strict rules of religion on others.

Chapter 5
The Return of Cheap Grace

1. For more on the subject of legalism see my book *Why Love Hates Legalism: An Irreverent Indictment of Mean Religion* (Lake Mary, FL: Creation House, 2015).
2. Dietrich Bonhoeffer, *The Cost of Discipleship* (New York: Macmillan, 1959).
3. *Merriam-Webster Online*, s.v. "antinomian," http://www.merriam-webster.com/dictionary/antinomian (accessed August 28, 2015).
4. I use "ministry monster" to refer to a ministry of man's own making. Leaders use manipulation and all manner of unethical means and gimmicks to raise funds and enlarge their ministries. A leader often expands and overextends himself—his ministry gets bigger than God ever intended and so the man has to sustain it without God's help. Like monsters, ministries demand more food as they get bigger. Unethical leaders, who are consumed with the task of feeding the monsters they made, lose sight of their true calling and compromise themselves in an effort to keep the monster alive. It eventually consumes them or leads to scandal or other calamity.

Chapter 6
Lying Signs and Wonders

1. *Dictionary.com*, s.v. "bona fide," http://dictionary.reference.com/browse/bona+fide (accessed August 28, 2015).
2. "False Lucy Rael: oil, stigmata, diamonds from Heaven," *Redeemed Hippie's Place* (blog), July 10, 2010,

https://redeemedhippiesplace.wordpress.com/2010/07/10/false-lucy-rael-oil-stigmata-diamonds-from-heaven/ (accessed August 25, 2015).

3. The Internet is filled with books and articles on Kundalini. It is most often experienced among Hindus. Simply defined, it is spiritual energy that lays dormant at the base of the spine until it is activated through yoga or the laying on of hands. I learned about it in my hippie days in Southern California from Krishna devotees and by reading Hindu writings, including those of the "Giggling Guru." Researching this subject is a complicated and laborious endeavor involving reading the writings of the "sages" from Eastern religions.

Chapter 7
It's Supernatural, Isn't It?

1. *Dictionary.com*, s.v. "weird," http://dictionary.reference.com/browse/weird (accessed August 25, 2015).
2. Dave Wilton, "Weird," February 17, 2007, *Word Origins*, http://www.wordorigins.org/index.php/site/comments/weird/ (accessed August 25, 2015).
3. Ibid.
4. *Dictionary.com*, s.v. "strange," http://dictionary.reference.com/browse/strange (accessed August 25, 2015).
5. *Merriam-Webster Online*, s.v. "strange," http://www.merriam-webster.com/dictionary/strange (accessed August 25, 2015).
6. *Collins*, s.v. "strange," http://www.collinsdictionary.com/dictionary/english/strange (accessed August 25, 2015).

7. "Vishnu," Religions, *BBC*, last modified August 24, 2009, http://www.bbc.co.uk/religion/religions/hinduism/deities/vishnu.shtml (accessed September 3, 2015).
8. *Merriam-Webster Online*, s.v. "avatar," http://www.merriam-webster.com/dictionary/avatar (accessed August 25, 2015).
9. Rishi Singh Gherwal, *Kundalini, The Mother of the Universe* (Santa Barbara, CA: R.S. Gherwal, 1930), http://www.sacred-texts.com/hin/kmu/kmu03.htm. Much of the book is long quotes of other Hindu writers.
10. Ibid.
11. *Dictionary.com*, s.v. "paranormal," http://dictionary.reference.com/browse/paranormal (accessed August 31, 2015).
12. Montrose Cunningham, "The 80s: 'Ghostbusters,'" *Soul Train* (blog), January 30, 2014, http://soultrain.com/2014/01/30/80s-ghostbusters/ (accessed August 25, 2015).
13. Gary L. Wood, *A Place Called Heaven* (Mustang, OK: Tate, 2008).

Chapter 8
Holy Laughter, Batman!

1. Sara Posner, "Newt Gingrich Visits the 'Holy Ghost Bartender,'" *Tampa Tribune*, August 8, 2012, http://religiondispatches.org/newt-gingrich-visits-the-holy-ghost-bartender/ (accessed September 3, 2015).
2. Nick Needham, "The Toronto Blessing," *The Shepherd* 16, parts 3, 4, and 5 (December 1995–February 1996), http://orthodoxinfo.com/inquirers/toronto.aspx (accessed September 3, 2015)

3. "David Wikerson's criticism of 'charasmatic' manifestations," YouTube video, 9:16, from a Moscow conference in 2000, posted by BigSmallVillage, July 26, 2008, https://www.youtube.com/watch?v=4gtTxrYtztQ.
4. Catch the Fire, "History," http://catchthefire.com/About/History (accessed May 20, 2015).
5. Lily Koppel, "Maharishi Mahesh Yogi, Spiritual Leader, Dies," *New York Times*, February 6, 2008, http://www.nytimes.com/2008/02/06/world/asia/06maharishi-1.html?=&_r=2& (accessed September 3, 2015).
6. See chapter 6, endnote 3.
7. John Wimber (founding leader of the Vineyard movement) from a letter responding to questions concerning some of the phenomena experienced in some Vineyard meetings, "John Wimber Responds to Phenomena," http://www.oocities.org/mhhahnza/Wimber.txt (accessed August 15, 2015). The "John Wimber Collection" containing Teachings as well as correspondence can be accessed at Regent University Library at http://www.regent.edu/lib/special-collections/wimber-collection.cfm.
8. Ibid.
9. Randy Clark's website, Global Awakening, found at https://globalawakening.com/home/about-global-awakening/history-of-global-awakening (accessed August 31, 2015.
10. See my books *Sacred Fire: Why Don't we Try Pentecost One More Time* and *Why Love hates Legalism: An Irreverent Indictment of Mean Religion*.
11. Steven Strang, "Floored in Toronto." *Charisma*, February, 1995, quoted in Albert James Dager, "Holy Laughter," http://www.rapidnet.com/~jbeard/bdm/Psychology/holylaugh.htm (accessed August 25, 2015).

12. He is in heaven now, but his newsletters and sermons are still available from World Challenge and Times Square Church at http://sermons.worldchallenge.org/pulpit_series_newsletters.
13. I believe the pastor he referred to is one who is often associated with holy laughter to this day; but I viewed him differently. He and the leaders associated with him corrected some of the behaviors characteristic of holy laughter and the Toronto Blessing. I was in several meetings at his church at different times and witnessed reverence for the Word of God. Clear messages came forth, distractions and disruptions during preaching were discouraged and dealt with, and multitudes went to the altar after clear presentations of Bible messages. For these and other reasons, I do not place the Brownsville revival in the same category as holy laughter and the Toronto Blessing; and therefore I do not address it in these pages.
14. "David Wikerson's criticism of 'charasmatic' manifestations."
15. Billy Brice, "David Wilkerson Blasts Faith Preachers in Sermon," *Charisma*, April 29, 2011 (originally published in the October 1999 issue of *Charisma*), http://www.charismamag.com/spirit/evangelism-missions/13383-david-wilkerson-blasts-faith-preachers-in-sermon (accessed August 31, 2015).
16. Ibid.
17. Ibid.
18. Ibid.
19. Ibid.
20. Ibid.

ABOUT THE AUTHOR

Ron Sutton was converted during the Jesus movement in 1972. He has ministered as a missionary, church planter, and evangelist throughout the USA, Africa, Latin America, Europe, and Asia. In addition to churches, he and his wife, Cindy, established several other ministries through the years, including a home for unwed mothers, a drug rehabilitation program, orphanages, and leaders' schools in Africa where Ron served as director of School of Christ International. His books on evangelism, pro-life pamphlets, and evangelistic literature have circulated worldwide. Ron continues to conduct meetings throughout the USA and internationally, while working on other books and assisting his son Ryan at The Grace Center, a dynamic, multicultural church in Festus, Missouri.

CONTACT THE AUTHOR

TO ORDER MATERIALS OR SCHEDULE MEETINGS

Address: The Grace Center
P.O. Box 21
Crystal City, Missouri 63019

Website: ronsuttonministries.com
or thegracecenter.com

Email: ronsutton49@yahoo.com

Phone: 314-960-8306